LILLIAN TOO'S

FENG SHUI YEAR

2002

LILLIAN TOO'S

FENG SHUI YEAR

2002

ELEMENT

Element

An Imprint of HarperCollinsPublishers
77–85 Fulham Palace Road
Hammersmith, London W6 8JB

The website address is: www.elementbooks.com

First published in Great Britain in 2001 by
Element Books Limited

10 9 8 7 6 5 4 3 2 1

Illustrations by Joan Corlass
Design by Ann Burnham

A catalogue record for this book
is available from the British Library

ISBN 0 00 712835-5

Printed and bound in Great Britain by
Scotprint, Haddington, East Lothian

Contents

Introduction

Feng shui is an amazingly fascinating practice that holds out the promise of tantalizing benefits for those who know how to use it correctly and smartly. Acceptance of feng shui is growing in the West, both among people of Western origins and a new generation of overseas Chinese who are rediscovering the seductive secrets of their heritage. As authentic Chinese feng shui grows in popularity, more of its secrets will be revealed to the English-speaking world. And as more and more people begin to understand the basics of feng shui – and experience and appreciate its potency – it becomes easier to disseminate the more advanced formulas.

There is a space and a time dimension to the practice of feng shui, and there is also an element of the scientific in feng shui calculations and in the use of the compass. Powerful compass formulas and annual updates, such as the information contained in this book, add substantially to the benefits of feng shui practice. In the same way as the compass aspect of its practice and the powerful symbolic side to its interpretation cannot be overlooked, neither can the effect of the passage of time on feng shui be ignored or underestimated.

Three Period Feng Shui

This book addresses the important time transformations of luck in the feng shui of buildings, based on the formulas of Three Period feng shui. The diagnosis and recommendations on remedies uses the powerful Flying Star and Eight Mansions formulas. I do not give detailed explanations of how the charts that contain the relevant information (referred to as natal charts) are derived, since this would turn the book into a cumbersome and complicated exercise in constructing charts and formulas. Instead everything has been made user-friendly.

This does not mean that I have simplified the formulas. What I have done is to organize my knowledge of the formulas and condense them into easy-to-understand charts and easy-to-follow tips on how you can assuage bad chi caused by time afflictions to your space, and also how you can take advantage of lucky stars flying into certain corners of your house. Everything contained in this book is aimed at ensuring you do not suffer from bad feng shui during the entire year of the water horse, but instead benefit by skillfully taking advantage of all the information that is revealed in the natal charts.

The explanations contained here have been simplified, but they still convey the essence of the nature of afflicted or auspicious energy being encountered. This, I believe, will allow any lay practitioner to make meaningful use of this book. I have made the explanations on remedies and cures much longer in response to requests from readers for me to be very detailed and exact when offering solutions to feng shui problems.

The Hsia Calender

This book focuses on the feng shui luck of houses in the year 2002, the year of the water horse. The calendar used in this book is generally referred to as the "Hsia" or "solar calender" of the Chinese calendar. It is different from the lunar calendar, which starts on a different day each year. The Hsia

	SE	S	SW	
	4	9	2	
E	3	5	7	W
	8	1	6	
	NE	N	NW	

This is the original Lo Shu square from which many feng shui formulas associated with compass directions are derived. Note the center number is 5 and that any three numbers in any direction add up to 15, which is the number of days of the moon's waxing or waning cycle. Hence the Lo Shu is the basis of time dimension feng shui.

calendar begins its year on the equivalent of either February 4 or 5 of the Gregorian calendar.

The Hsia calendar is used when analyzing the effect of time on feng shui. Each Hsia year and month has a ruling *Lo Shu* square, and it is the numbers and their sequential placement in this square that is the basis of time dimension feng shui. Familiarize yourself with the *Lo Shu* square shown here.

How To Use This Book

There are two steps to practicing time dimension feng shui.

The first step is to learn how to diagnose the nature of the afflictions that you will experience during the course of the year, based on the chart of your house. So in this first stage you will be developing familiarity with what are termed the "natal charts" of buildings.

There are different types of natal charts. Since feng shui is such an old science its journey down the centuries, in a country split by regional dialects and interpretations, has not been without its share of controversy in interpretation. Today we also have feng shui masters who disagree (with different degrees of dogmatism) with each other as to how natal charts should be constructed and interpreted.

This book addresses two different natal charts.

The first set of natal charts divides all buildings into eight categories. Under this system, buildings (or houses) are categorized according to what is termed their sitting trigram. Since there are eight trigrams, there are deemed to be eight categories of buildings. These buildings are called *Kan, Li, Chen, Tui, Sun, Kun, Chien,* and *Ken* houses. Each of these eight houses is affected differently by the annual 2002 chart. There is therefore a full set of readings for these houses. Readers can start to investigate their house feng shui for 2002 based on this set of readings.

The second set of natal charts is more detailed and complex. It offers scope for more information to be analyzed, and is a deeper investigation into the nuances of luck in each sector of the home. In this system, there are actually a total of 144 natal charts of houses. These charts are based on nine time periods, each lasting 20 years. Within each period there are 16 categories of houses.

We are currently in the Period of 7, so the detailed readings of the 16 houses belonging to this current period are given. Under this system, which is the Flying Star system of feng shui, houses are categorized according to their direction. There are sixteen categories of directions, and thus 16 different natal charts.

Buildings (and houses) constructed or renovated between February 4, 1984 and February 4, 2004 are considered to be period 7 houses. The period of 7 comes to an end on February 4, 2004, so the influence of number 7 – which is very lucky during the period of 7 – is beginning to wane. After 2004 the period number changes to 8, so 8 – a very lucky number even before the period of 8 – becomes even luckier as we draw closer to 2004.

The second step in using this book is to identify the danger sectors of your house during 2002. Each year the danger sectors of every house - and the auspicious corners as well – undergo subtle changes.

Please note that almost all branches of Chinese esoteric practices believe in the tenet that "prevention is infinitely better than cure." As such, the motivation behind this book is to alert you to sectors that are afflicted. You should thus identify these sectors, based on the information given here, and take the recommended measures to prevent yourself from falling ill, losing a loved one, meeting with accidents, and suffering substantial financial losses. You should first take note of the major annual afflictions.

Feng Shui Annual Afflictions

When you know which sectors of your home or office are afflicted in 2002, you will be in a position to ensure that you do not inadvertently get hit by the intangible forces caused by so-called "bad flying stars" and afflictions in the annual *Lo Shu* chart of 2002. These "stars" fly in and out of living spaces, bringing problems wherever they temporarily settle. They must be treated with respect since the misfortune they cause is usually severe. Basically there are three main types of annual feng shui afflictions:

✵ The Grand Duke Jupiter (also known in Chinese as the *Tai Sui*)
✵ The Three Killings affliction
✵ The Flying Star Five Yellow

Each year you should be wary of the sectors, or palaces, that are affected by afflictions and by the five yellow. You will also be warned about taboos relating to undertaking renovations, shifting house and generally disturbing the energy of these afflicted sectors. I have included previously unrevealed remedies to deal with the resulting bad feng shui caused by breaking these taboos. If, for instance, you have incurred the wrath of the Grand Duke Jupiter by disturbing his palace during the year, you can at least mitigate the severity of his wrath by implementing some cures.

It cannot be overemphasized, however, that prevention is better than cure. In Hong Kong, feng shui masters offer personalized readings of their customers' homes at the start of each New Year to ensure that their feng shui luck stays intact throughout the year. It is necessary to do this at the start of the year to spell out exactly what residents should avoid doing throughout the year.

It is easy to be affected by misfortune if one is unaware of the taboos to observe, since they override any kind of good feng shui of your home or office building. If you do not take note of annual flying stars, and how to avoid misfortunes caused by them, you could suffer from accidents, losses, mishaps, and a great deal of bad luck without even knowing why. This is because we are not dealing with spatial concepts, but with the intangible forces of time dimension feng shui.

This naturally adds a fresh new angle to the practice of feng shui. The year 2002 is the year of the water horse and, based on the reading of the year's annual chart, the indications are that it is going to be a challenging year. The elements of the year are fire and water; two elements that are in direct conflict with each other. There are other interesting indications as well, so I urge you to read on. Pay careful attention to the sections of the text that deal with remedies and cures. This is a year when you must be defensive. You must have the remedies in place.

Lillian Too
Kuala Lumpur, May 2001

PART ONE

THE ANNUAL LO SHU CHART FOR THE YEAR 2002

The Annual Lo Shu Chart

The luck of all houses is affected by the annual *Lo Shu* chart (the annual chart for 2002 is illustrated below). In the year 2002, the ruling number is 7 so the *Lo Shu* chart for the year has 7 in the center. This chart illustrates the distribution of *chi* in each of the nine grids, which are referred to as palaces in the classical texts. You can see that because the ruling number changes each year, so too will the ruling *Lo Shu* chart, and so too will the distribution of *chi*. This has both good and bad effects on the luck of houses and businesses, depending on their particular natal chart, which in turn depends on two things – one, the door and house orientations, and two, when the house was built or last renovated.

The analysis of the luck of buildings in any year is based on the way the numbers fly into the nine grids in that year. If you examine the year 2002 *Lo Shu* chart, you will note that in this year the annual chart repeats the

☆ **NOTE:** In accordance with the tradition adopted in Chinese feng shui texts, the *Lo Shu* and *Pa Kua* grids are always drawn with south on top. In practice, of course, you should use a good compass to identify each of the directions. Also, in your analysis of your own home, you might want to re-orientate the *Lo Shu* square such that the top is facing your door direction so that the whole grid fits the orientation of your own home. This will make your analysis a lot easier.

southeast	south	southwest
6 LUCKY STAR	2 GRAND DUKE	4 LUCKY STAR
east	2002	west
5 FIVE YELLOW	7	9 EXPANDING STAR
northeast	north	northwest
1 LUCKY STAR	3 3 KILLINGS FIGHTING STAR	8 VERY AUSPICIOUS

period chart. This is because the ruling number of both the year 2002 and the current period is the same – it is the number 7. This means that the effect of the different numbers flying into the different grids is doubly strong. Auspicious numbers therefore become very auspicious, while unlucky numbers will be very troublesome for the sector they occupy.

You will also note that the lucky numbers 8 and 6 are in the northwest and southeast respectively. This makes the NW/SE axis very auspicious, and all houses sitting on this axis will enjoy good luck for the year. What this means is that houses that have a regular shape and face either northwest or southeast with a proper front and back door will enjoy good fortune. Another way of interpreting this is that all houses with entrance doors located in the northwest or southeast grids will also enjoy good luck.

While I have indicated that the numbers 6 and 8 are auspicious, please note that the meanings or attributes of all the nine numbers change according to different circumstances and factors.

These factors are summarized as follows:

☆ **The Period** – each period lasts for 20 years. We are now in the period of 7, which started on February 4, 1984 and will end on February 3, 2004. The next period is the period of 8, which begins on February 4, 2004. In each period, the individual star numbers assert different types of *chi* and therefore create different scenarios of luck. Some star numbers have different meanings in different periods. Thus, the number 7 is extremely lucky in this period of 7 but it turns terribly unlucky and indicates great violence during the coming period of 8.

☆ **The Palace**, or sector, which the star number flies into. Whenever we speak of palace we are referring to one of the nine compass sectors of the *Lo Shu* grid. There are nine palaces in all, and each palace is said to have its own attributes, characteristics, and elements. For instance, the auspicious star number 6 will have a different effect and luck when it flies into the east palace than when it flies into the southeast palace.

NOTE:

The nine star numbers
of the Flying Star
system of feng shui are
the numbers 1 to 9.
By understanding their
meanings, feng shui
analysis of buildings
and periods can be
considerably enhanced.
It is therefore worth
the effort to understand
these numbers as
thoroughly as possible
from the outset.

✫ **The Natal Star Number** in the palace where it flies to. For instance, when the auspicious star 6 flies into the southeast of your house, it is necessary to examine the flying star natal chart of your house in order to gauge its impact. What are referred to as the "mountain star" and the "water star" of your southeast palace need to be investigated. These are the natal chart stars. They are also referred to as the sitting stars and the facing stars respectively. The mountain star is the sitting star and the water star is the facing star. If you are reading about stars in feng shui for the first time, it will seem very complicated but bear with me. It really is very simple once you become familiar with the different terms. Mountain and water star feng shui is pretty powerful stuff and is part of the Flying Star system, so it's worthwhile familiarizing yourself with it.

✫ **The Annual Star and Monthly Stars** exert varying effects on different palaces. Thus, while a star number may be generally auspicious or inauspicious, the exact nature and degree of the luck it brings will differ depending on which palace it flies into. You therefore need to know which numbers are deemed to be lucky and which are deemed to be unlucky. In addition, while single numbers offer a general indication of luck, it is really the combination of numbers that exerts the strongest effect on the *chi*.

This illustration shows the planetary stars of the Sickle, which are said to be the basis of the star numbers. The white stars numbered 1, 6, and 8 are the auspicious stars. The 3 jade star and 4 green star have different attributes under different circumstances. The 5 yellow star and 2 black star are evil stars bringing illness and death. The 7 red brings violence. The 9 purple brings a magnification of both good and bad.

The nine numbers are often described in terms of the nine stars of the Ursa Major, which in reality only has 7 stars. The configuration of stars is illustrated in the sketch opposite. For the purposes of feng shui, two extra stars are added at the tail of the configuration.

The attributes of each of the star numbers evolve and change according to different periods. Having said that, however, the numbers 1, 6, and 8 are always regarded as auspicious. The difference during each period is in the intensity of good fortune indicated, as well as the types of good fortune which they each bring. In the same way, the stars 2, 5, and 3 are always regarded with a great deal of wariness since they often create problems.

The numbers also take on extra or diminished attributes according to whether they are water stars or mountain stars, and depending on how they interact with each other. Thus, for instance, the number 9 is a fullness star which is also independent. It enhances both good and bad luck stars. With the 5 it makes bad luck worse. With the 8 it makes good luck even better.

SE	S	SW
6	2	4
5	7	9
(1)	3	8
NE	N	NW

E (left side) · W (right side)

☆ The White Star Number One is in the Northeast in 2002

The number 1 is generally considered an auspicious star number in any chart. It brings opportunities, new beginnings, and academic and literary success. It also indicates good career opportunities.

In the year 2002, the 1 star enters the northeast palace. This is the place of the trigram *Ken*, the mountain, which indicates a hidden storehouse of wealth and assets. Thus it is called the "Later Heaven connection." This means the 1 (of the annual star) has entered the 8 palace (8 is the basic number of the northeast palace in the original *Lo Shu* square).

The meeting of 1 with 8 suggests good fortune during the entire year of 2002 for anyone who has their room in the northeast sector. Good fortune in this instance will come in the form of excellent exam grades, success in all kinds of literary pursuits, gains in financial investments, and smooth sailing in your job and career. It also benefits those houses whose main door is located in the northeast palace.

While the combination generally indicates good fortune for the northeast palace, additional analysis must be undertaken by examining the element interaction between the numbers, the natal charts of the house, and also by examining the *Lo Shu* chart on a month-by-month basis for the year. These additional investigations will fine-tune the analysis and offer better clues on how to enhance the luck of the northeast further and how to avoid the bad months.

The 1 star flying into the northeast also indicates that those engaged in the oil, water, liquid, property, research, and other earth-related fields will enjoy extremely good fortune. These businesses benefit enormously from this auspicious combination in the northeast.

The negative side of the 1 star flying into the 8 base has to do with the effect of the elements interacting. Water and earth are not friends. In this case the element of water is flying into the mountain of earth, suggesting an overflow. There could be hidden and unexpected danger indicated, so anyone with a room here is advised to be careful about taking on risks, or of trusting people. Water overcoming earth always suggests a relationship going sour.

Those engaged in people-related jobs or those who are at school or in college should be careful not to overstress themselves.

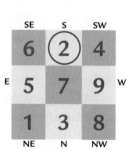

SE	S	SW
6	2	4
5	7	9
1	3	8
NE	N	NW

E (left) · W (right)

☆ The Black Star Number Two is in the South in 2002

The number 2 is the original malignant star, which does not bode well for anyone or any house in almost any period. In the present period of 7, it is regarded as the "monarch of sickness" and its presence brings illness, disease, and distress associated with ill health.

During the year 2002, the 2 black star flies into the south palace. This is the place of the *Li* trigram, which signifies fire. This trigram indicates supreme *yang* energy. Its base number is 9, the magnifying star. The combination of these two numbers strengthens the malignant 2 and gives it added power.

The interpretation of 2 flying into the south is earth flying into fire. Earth exhausts fire so the 2 star brings a great deal of stress and sickness to anyone residing in this sector. It threatens illness to middle-aged women, especially if they happen to be staying in the south palace of their homes. It is a good idea to ensure that women in the family avoid exposing themselves to infectious diseases.

The combination of the black 2 star with the base 9 star creates what is referred to as the "Later Heaven Fire formation," which indicates misfortunes related to the loss of one's good name and honor.

The 2 star poses the greatest danger in the eleventh month, when both the month and year star, as well as the period star, has the preponderance of 2. The eleventh month falls between December 7 and January 6. In this month anyone who has a bedroom in the south is strongly advised to sleep in another bedroom or on the sofa in the living room. Otherwise they stand a real risk of getting very ill.

The combination of 2 and base 9 also suggests that the south palace has become hot-blooded and unbalanced. So if your office is located in the south sector of the building, you might find yourself getting into arguments, legal disputes, and quarrels that could lead to loss. Misunderstandings arise from competitive pressures and business rivalries. It is wise to be extra careful and avoid taking too many risks.

At home, please note that during certain months this star brings sickness to those born under KUA numbers 1, 3, 4, and 9 (see page 253); those people who are categorized as east-group people – i.e. people who benefit from facing and sitting in the north and south. This is because the south palace, being afflicted, sends out killing energy to east-group people who would, under normal circumstances, benefit hugely from sitting in the south and facing north (or vice versa since south is an auspicious direction for them).

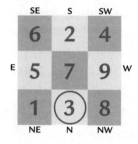

SE	S	SW
6	2	4
5	7	9
1	(3)	8
NE	N	NW

☆ The Jade Star Number Three is in the North in 2002

The 3 star – jade – is regarded as the evil star of disputes and quarrels. During this period, the 3 star is responsible for bickering, disagreements, and litigation. If it flies into a bedroom, a great deal of agitation will arise between members of the same household.

In the year 2002 – the year of the water horse – this horrible star flies into the palace of the north, thereby bringing its evil influence to anyone who has a bedroom here or, worse, anyone whose main front door is located here. At its worst the 3 star brings costly and lengthy lawsuits that threaten significant loss.

The 3 star is regarded as an unfortunate star, which should generally be avoided. Sometimes, however, it can bring good fortune as it did during the year of the dragon in 2000, when it flew into the northeast. That was an auspicious combination based on Early Heaven analysis, since the combination of 3 annual star with the 8 base star indicated growth and auspicious new beginnings.

In this year of the water horse, the 3 star has flown into the north, where the base number is 1. This combination suggests exhaustion. Quarrels leading to a sense of defeat and failure, weariness, and despair is the result. This is because the 3 star is wood and coming into the palace of the water star the effect is exhaustion. Thus those staying in the north palace sector should note that all misunderstandings and hostility that plague them during the year will lead to exhaustion and defeat.

Residents of the north palace are especially vulnerable during the eleventh month, when the 3 becomes dominant. Care should also be taken during the ninth and twelfth months, when the 5 and 2 stars visit the north palace. Accidents and illness arising from quarrels and anger may occur. This is especially true for children under the age of twelve.

The combination of 3 with 2 which happens in the twelfth month (between January 6 and February 4, 2003) is an especially trying time. There will be unexplained temper tantrums, and relationships between residents living in the same house will be very hostile. Relationships with outsiders are also in for a hard time.

Those whose master bedroom is in the north should simply sleep in another room during this month. At work, anyone sharing an office in the north will experience conflicts so severe they could lead to permanent rifts.

☆ The Green Star Number Four is in the Southwest in 2002

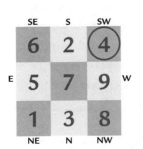

Generally speaking, the green 4 star governs romance and academic advancement during the period of 7. It is usually associated with creativity, workmanship, and great inventiveness. The 4 star also usually brings interesting new people on the romantic front.

In the year 2002, the 4 star flies to the southwest palace, which instantly indicates that the southwest palace will enjoy very powerful *chi* of romance and love luck. So if your door is located in the southwest in 2002, the 4 star could bring a great deal of both wanted and unwanted romantic opportunities to everyone in the house. If you occupy a bedroom in the southwest sector, you will surely have plenty of romance in your life in the year 2002.

So, depending on your current marital status, it is a good idea to be extra watchful, especially during the eleventh month i.e. between December 7 and January 6. Those who are single are likely to meet potential soul mates during this month, while those who are married could well be starting an affair – especially if there is water in the southwest of their homes! Whether this ultimately represents good or bad luck depends on your particular circumstances.

You should also note that the 4 star is of the wood element and flying into the southwest indicates that the wood is coming in to hurt the earth of the southwest. So while romance may be in the air, it could also be bringing trouble as well – especially for the woman, who is the most likely to get hurt. It might be better to focus on the other great benefit brought by the 4 star number – its positive effect on those in the writing and

2002

Feng Shui year 2002

educational fields. Authors and teachers will enjoy excellent luck from the southwest during the year. In the same way, career and business people who can successfully energize the *chi* from the southwest will also enjoy promotions and enhanced incomes.

There is a negative aspect to the 4 star and this has to do with betrayal, humiliation in affairs of the heart, sex scandals, and heartbreak. The 4 star brings heartbreak, especially when the monthly 3, 5, or 7 stars visit. The worst time will be when the monthly 5 visits, during the month of November (between November 7 and December 7). So if your room is located in the southwest, borrow one of your siblings' rooms if you are starting a love affair. This is the correct way of escaping the inauspicious combination of the 4 and 5. If you have any kind of water feature in the southwest this year it is a good idea to remove it temporarily since water here leads to severe problems related to infidelity and betrayal.

☆ The Yellow Star Number Five is in the East in 2002

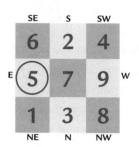

The 5 yellow is the most dangerous star number in the *San Yuan* system of feng shui. The 5 yellow star is unlucky, inauspicious, and causes a variety of misfortunes under almost all circumstances.

In the year 2002, the 5 yellow flies to the east palace with the effect that it "plants a time bomb in the east," which will explode when and if certain things occur. The best way to treat the 5 yellow is simply to leave it well alone. It should thus be avoided and left undisturbed. It is, most of all, to be feared, so from the start of the year remedial action needs be taken to ensure it is kept under control.

This is because, if activated, the 5 yellow is capable of causing massive problems. This is one star that can really bring serious calamities and a great deal of ill fortune. These manifestations of bad luck range from major injuries sustained in serious accidents to illnesses that can be fatal. It can also cause disharmony, disrupt business plans, cause rifts in relationships, and be the source of disputes and losses.

In the year of the water horse, the 5 yellow is not at the height of its negative power. This is because flying into the east, the 5 of earth meets the 3 of wood and wood is capable of destroying earth.

Thus, when the 5 yellow star enters the east palace, the effect is that "the killing force of the army is itself killed," indicating that its effect is less serious and severe than in other years. The force of 5's bad earth *chi* on the 3 base star, which signifies the element of wood, reflects the destructive cycle of the elements. According to the theory of the five elements, wood destroys earth - thankfully here it is the 5 earth that gets destroyed.

So the 5 star coming into the east does not have enough strength to destroy the *chi* of the east palace. There is thus less danger from the 5 this year. Nevertheless, care should be taken during certain months; particularly August, when the month star of 9 flies in to enhance the 5 yellow and seriously weaken the base wood star. In August (between August 8 and September 8), anyone staying in an east room could fall ill so it is better to move out of the room during this time.

Another month when there could be problems is December, when the 5 is strengthened by the month star which, is also 5.

☆ The White Star Number Six is in the Southeast in 2002

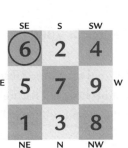

The 6 white star is extremely auspicious. It signifies great achievements – the attainment of great power, authority, and high rank. The 6 star is considered to be extremely lucky in many different scenarios. Its presence in any palace should always be energized and activated correctly for it to bring great feng shui.

In the year 2002, the 6 white star has flown to the southeast – an occurrence which signifies "heaven falling into the lap of the eldest daughter." This is because the 6 white star represents heaven and the trigram *Chien*, while the 4 of the southeast signifies the eldest daughter. This is indicated by the trigram *Sun*. The coming together of *Chien* with *Sun* spells exceptional good fortune coming to the eldest (or only) daughters of families.

In 2002, if your door is oriented to face southeast or is located in the southeast, the family – particularly the women – will enjoy excellent good fortune, especially in the area of career and business success, as well as in the attainment of power and influence. The 6 star indicates all these things.

The 6 white star is an intrinsically lucky star, especially in the area of material and worldly pursuits. It is lucky in both the period of 7 and in the forthcoming period of 8. This star is also excellent for those who are spiritually inclined or who are deeply religious. Those engaged in the metaphysical fields will enjoy good fortune in terms of attaining positive realizations, spiritual awakening, and wisdom.

The negative note of the 6 star is that, while it represents attainment and wealth, it also symbolizes loneliness and a tendency toward the solitary state. Those who enjoy the good fortune of the 6 star in the southeast during the year of the horse will find themselves feeling lonely and depressed during the months of July and January the following year, but such feelings are short-lived. In those months wear lots of gold and diamond jewelry (the real thing), as this counters such feelings of despondency.

More serious will be the feeling of being stabbed in the back and betrayed that will afflict those residing in the southeast during the month of June 2002. These emotionally-charged delusions will cause unhappiness, but these too will pass.

☆ The Red Star Number Seven is in the Center in 2002

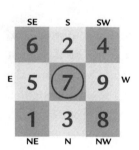

The 7 star is also the *Lo Shu* number of the year. The 7 red star is the most auspicious star during the period of 7, but it has an inherently evil nature! It is lucky only during this period. Once we enter the period of 8, it will manifest its true nature, which signifies armed assault, violence, and robbery.

Throughout the current 20-year period, however, the 7 star is most auspicious, heralding great prosperity as well as wonderful achievements and happiness. Thus the 7 star is considered auspicious wherever it appears in the natal chart of period 7 houses.

The annual 7 star, however, exerts different types of *chi* depending on which palace it enters. In the year 2002 it has flown into the center palace, so broadly speaking it brings general good chi to all houses during the year. Based on this alone, it is possible to say that finances will be good and lifestyle will be affluent. Alas, however, we are now nearing the tail end of the reign of 7 – its power is waning and its *chi* is weak. As such, it is considered that it does not have the strength to overcome other bad indications for the year. It cannot overcome, for instance, the clash of elements indicated by the heavenly stem (water) and the earthly branch (fire) of the year 2002.

Also, in terms of health, the 7 star red coming to the center does not generally bode well for anyone. This is because here we see metal star coming into a place of earth. The center of the home is signified by the earth element. So the center of the home is exhausted by the 7. In the cycle of the five elements, metal exhausts earth. Since the center palace affects the whole household, the 7 star flying here afflicts everyone.

The 7 star will favor entrepreneurship and businesses that are engaged in jewelry-making, art, and craftsmanship. Those involved in such businesses should do well during the year if the center part of their home is clearly visible. This means if it falls into the living room of the home.

Meanwhile, I'd like to sound a warning note on the possibility of robbery. During the months of October and December it is a good idea to be extra careful when going out, since the likelihood of robberies is quite high. And because the 7 star is usually associated with armed robbery, it is advisable to remember that should anything negative occur, it is better to lose money than to lose limbs or even one's life.

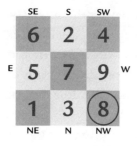

	SE	S	SW	
	6	2	4	
E	5	7	9	W
	1	3	8	
	NE	N	NW	

☆ The White Star Number Eight is in the Northwest in 2002

This is the third white star in the system and is generally regarded as the luckiest and most auspicious of all the nine stars. The 8 white star governs the luck of wealth, distinction, prosperity, prestige, and great success.

During this period the 8 white star is already auspicious and signifies coming prosperity. However, when we reach the period of 8 in the year 2004, the star 8 will be so enormously auspicious that anyone who succeeds in tapping it correctly and effectively will enjoy tremendous wealth. By then it will mean "current prosperity."

Many feng shui books suggest that those born with KUA number 8 will enjoy tremendous good luck during the coming period of 8. KUA numbers are calculated using one's year of birth and gender, and are part of the Eight Mansions school of feng shui (see page 253 for the KUA formula.)

During the year 2002, the year of the water horse, the auspicious 8 annual star flies to the northwest, the place of the father, the patriarch, and also the place of heaven. During the year this sector – the northwest – is the luckiest sector of all the nine sectors of the grid. This is mainly due to the star 8 having flown here and the combination of elements and numbers that result from it.

So anyone who has their living room, bedroom, main door, or office in the northwest sector will benefit from the 8 star. It brings great good fortune and exciting times. The base number of the northwest is 6 and since 6 and 8 are both white numbers they are immediately compatible. Also, 6 is metal and 8 is earth. So earth coming into metal produces it – under the cycle of the five elements theory, there is nothing more auspicious!

Here the significance is that of a "whole mountain" of wealth coming into the northwest, the place where gold or metal is the dominant element. This indicates that the patriarch of the family benefits greatly from the year if his room is also located in the northwest corner of his home or if the door is placed in the northwest. The most auspicious month of the year for this corner is December, but October and May are also very good months for the northwest. There is plenty of good fortune indicated. There will also be many opportunities that lead to the building of sizeable assets.

There are no negative notes to the star 8, and it is recommended that homes which have a northwest facing door or which are oriented northwest should consider activating the 8 white star by placing a water feature there. Even if it is only for a year, the water feature will bring great good luck, and if the stars of the natal chart also indicate an auspicious configuration of stars for the northwest, then you should definitely have a water feature.

Those of you who implement this suggestion should feel the difference in your income and wealth luck very quickly indeed. This is the year to strike it big.

☆ **The Purple Star Number Nine is in the West in 2002**

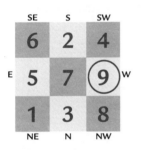

The 9 purple star is an extraordinary star which has many layers and nuances of meanings. In the year 2002 it enters the west palace of any home or building. This means that during the course of the year its major attributes will affect those houses whose front door faces the west or are located in the west corner of the house. It also means that those houses with a lucky configuration of lucky flying star numbers in the west grid will have their good fortune enhanced, while those houses with an unfortunate configuration of flying stars in the west will have their bad luck magnified.

This is because the 9 star is generally considered to be an unstable star. It is a star which heralds a great many changes, both of the heavenly as well as the earthly kind. The reason for this is that the 9 star signifies the fullness of heaven and earth's good luck, as well as the fullness of heaven and earth's bad luck.

The 9 purple star exerts auspicious influences when in the company of auspicious stars, and it causes killing *chi* to magnify when in the presence of unlucky stars. Many classical texts on Flying Star feng shui refer to the 9 star as the "master of volatility and change."

There is an advanced branch of Flying Star techniques known as the Purple White scripts.

These techniques focus on the application and uses of the white star numbers with the purple star number. We have seen that the three white stars 1, 6, and 8 are the lucky stars of the system. When the 9 star is added in, the good fortune is said to be immeasurably and very considerably enhanced.

So the auspicious months for the year 2002 will be June (June 6 to July 7), November (November 7 to December 7), and January 2003 (January 6 to February 4). These are the months when the month stars of 1,6, and 8 will combine with the 9 purple star in the west. Those with rooms in this sector should take note.

On the other hand, when the 9 star is combined with either or several of the yellow or black stars the result is acute danger. Thus in the year 2002 the months to watch out for will be July (July 7 to August 8) and October (October 8 to November 7). These two months are the generally unfavorable months for those residing in the west during the year 2002.

Element Analysis of the 2002 Feng Shui Chart

The element analysis of the 2002 Feng Shui chart will reveal a great deal of information about the luck of houses. This is because in addition to their intrinsic meanings, the numbers 1 to 9 also represent the five elements. Each number symbolizes one of the five elements. Since so many of feng shui's secrets are connected to the way the elements are said to interact with one another to produce a variety of outcomes, Flying Star and Eight Mansions feng shui also lean heavily on the theory of the five elements when determining the effects of star numbers and directions. It is therefore important to understand the interaction of elements that takes place each time a number flies into a sector of the superimposed Lo Shu grid.

Once you understand that the Lo Shu grid of numbers also symbolizes elements, it reveals a great deal about the nature of luck as it transforms from year to year, and from month to month.

The Theory of Five Elements

The theory of five elements revolves around the elements of wood, fire, earth, metal, and water. These elements have three cyclical relationships with each other and it is important to develop an easy familiarity with these cycles if you want to understand both feng shui analysis and the basis of most feng shui cures.

The three cycles of the five elements are:

- ✬ The productive and hence auspicious cycle
- ✬ The destructive and thus inauspicious cycle
- ✬ The exhaustive cycle, which is excellent for applying feng shui cures

The productive cycle generally shows the elements that have a balanced and harmonious relationship. Any element that enhances (produces) the element represented by your space (as determined by the compass direction) is generally considered auspicious and lucky.

Anything belonging to an element that destroys the element represented by your space (your space can be your room or your door location) is usually regarded as being unlucky and inauspicious.

So the key to understanding feng shui is quite simple. Develop an awareness of the elements and develop a sensitivity to everything you see in any space. You must, of course, arm yourself with a compass. Feng shui is all about compass directions.

It is the orientation of any given space that gives meaning to the way *chi* flows, and by extension to all feng shui analysis and cures. It is simply impossible to conceive of anyone practicing feng shui without using the compass. This is because at the heart of feng shui, as it has been practiced over the past few thousand years, is the compass. All the formulas are expressed in terms of the directions of the compass.

It is the same with the elements. The five element theory is the bridge between understanding orientations and everything that affects the energy of these orientations. This is how space is defined – in terms of the orientations as determined by a compass.

To enable you to develop an easy familiarity with the elements, look at the diagram reproduced on the opposite page. It shows the five elements arranged in a circular flow, with a star in the center. The circular flow going clockwise shows the productive flow cycle of the elements. So wood produces fire, which produces earth, which produces metal, which produces water, which produces wood, and so the cycle goes in a never-ending circular flow.

The counter-clockwise flow shows the exhaustive cycle. So when wood produces fire, it also means fire exhausts wood. So wood exhausts water, and water exhausts metal, and metal exhausts earth, and earth exhausts fire, and so on.

The star in the center shows the destructive cycle of the elements.

This illustrates that fire destroys metal and metal destroys wood. Wood destroys earth, and earth destroys water which destroys fire.

Remember this table and commit the three fundamental relationships to memory.

Next familiarize yourself with the relationship between numbers and elements. Each number stands for an element. And at the same time each direction also stands for an element. This is summarized below. These simple and straightforward pieces of information are the building blocks to understanding basic feng shui. When you understand these fundamentals you will have a sound basis that will enable you to grasp everything else you read after this. So:

☆ 1 is north and water
☆ 9 is south and fire
☆ 2, 5, and 8 are earth; so southwest, center, and northeast are earth
☆ 3 and 4 are wood, so east and southeast are wood
☆ 6 and 7 are metal, so northwest and west are metal

Knowing these simple correlations will help you to understand the rationale that lies behind the readings, as well as the basic principles that underscore the remedies recommended. And then, with experience, you will very quickly develop an understanding and a feel for the numbers and their meanings.

The directions also have other attributes that can be used to gain a deeper analysis of the numbers and their meanings. These are laid out in the shape of the *Pa Kua*, which expresses all the attributes associated with the eight directions. Keep this as a useful tool to aid you in understanding the readings given later in the book. Do not expect to know everything immediately. These basic fundamentals are explained in greater detail in my earlier books on feng shui. They are summarized here mainly to help those new to feng shui appreciate the basis of the readings and the cures suggested.

Having said that I would like to make two additional statements:

Firstly, that these basic tools do not explain everything. There is a great deal more to feng shui but these basic fundamentals provide an excellent framework for analysis.

Secondly, that there are "exceptions" to the rule – not because they are exceptions as such, but because one must think deeply to really understand feng shui at subtle levels.

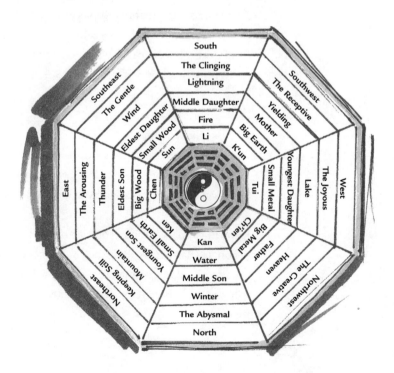

For example, while water destroys fire, a little bit of water and fire under certain circumstances turns into steam which is power! Also, while metal destroys wood, under some circumstances metal gives greater value to the wood, as with a piece of furniture for instance.

So it is necessary to be smart in your practice of feng shui.

Common sense plays a big part in creating good feng shui and avoiding bad feng shui!

The 2002 Annual Chart

Year 2002 –

The Water Horse

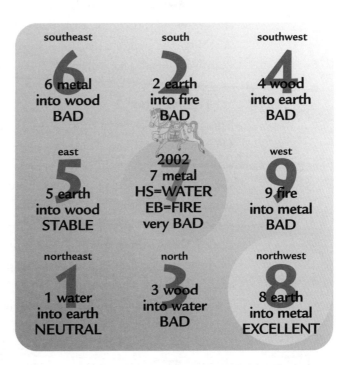

southeast	south	southwest
6 6 metal into wood BAD	**2** 2 earth into fire BAD	**4** 4 wood into earth BAD
east **5** 5 earth into wood STABLE	2002 7 metal HS=WATER EB=FIRE very BAD	west **9** 9 fire into metal BAD
northeast **1** 1 water into earth NEUTRAL	north **3** 3 wood into water BAD	northwest **8** 8 earth into metal EXCELLENT

☆ The Number 7

The chart on the previous page summarizes the interaction of the elements in the year 2002 based on how the star numbers fly from grid to grid. This year the center reigning Lo Shu number is 7. This means that 7 metal has flown into the center earth. It is important to be careful about which element is flying in, and which element is the base. So in this case the center grid, the core of the building, has a base element of earth. The 7 star number flies in in 2002 so metal comes in. Metal exhausts earth, so generally speaking the effect is not good. Therefore the first thing this says about 2002 is that it will be an exhausting year for many people.

Remedy for the center: In the year 2002, strengthen the earth element of the center of your home with fire energy. Use lights, lamps, candles – anything that suggests the fire element. Fire will strengthen earth while destroying metal. This will help you overcome the lethargy of the year.

☆ The Number 2

This number has flown into the south signifying earth flying into fire. Once again this is bad. This is because earth exhausts fire. The *chi* of the south is also exhausted by the year's flying star number. It does not indicate good things for anyone with a door in the south or with a room here. This also means that for the year in question if the south is your direction and it is an important direction for your home (e.g. if the door is placed there), then anything you undertake this year will be most exhausting. Whether or not you succeed depends on other indications, but residents of such a home will be tired out. In addition, as we have seen, the 2 star is an illness star. So bad luck is indicated for the south sector.

Remedy for the south: To overcome the afflictions of the south sector in the year 2002, you must use plants which give out the energy of wood. Place lots of fresh flowers and healthy growing plants in the south. This will strengthen the fire while overcoming the earth element. This remedy will clear away all exhaustion.

☆ The Number 3

This number has flown into the north. This indicates wood flying into water – once again an exhausting impact and this time on the north. The effect on houses with their main doors located in the north is very negative in that it suggests being under pressure and succumbing to being tired and overworked. Those living in this part of the house should take care not to overdo things. Overwork will have unhappy consequences.

Remedy for the north: To overcome the affliction of the north caused by the annual flying star, you should use metal windchimes. Hang several six-rod metal windchimes in the north. You can also place six coins under the carpet and over the doorway. The metal energy produces water and annihilates the offending wood energy in the north.

☆ The Number 4

This flies into the southwest. In element terms this means wood flying into earth – a destructive effect. Wood destroys earth in the cycle. The impact on those with doors in the southwest is that the base element is under attack. If your room is here or if your front door is located here you must do something to overcome the bad element interaction of the 4 coming in.

Remedy for the southwest: In the year 2002 you must keep lots of bright lights turned on in the southwest of your home. More so if your front door is placed there. This is an excellent way to overcome bad luck caused by the negative element interactions of the flying stars. Fire energy will exhaust the wood while strengthening earth.

☆ The Number 5

This flies into the east. Earth into wood means the elements are not in severe conflict and the situation is stable. The problem, of course, is that 5 is the deadly Five Yellow, which under normal circumstances brings enormous bad luck. In the east, however, it is kept under control by the wood energy, since earth is destroyed by wood. Windchimes – the usual remedy for the Five

Yellow – cannot be used here in the east because the metal energy will hurt the wood element. So do not hang windchimes in the east.

Remedy for the east: Strengthen wood energy in the east part of the house with lots of plants. This will ensure that the Five Yellow is kept on a tight rein.

☆ The Number 6

This number flies into the southeast, signifying metal flying into wood. This element relationship is severely destructive. Although 6 is an auspicious star, the impact of the elements suggests otherwise. What this is interpreted to mean is that good luck brought by the flying star transforms into misfortune. The analysis so far suggests that 2002 is not going to be a good year at all. Even the good stars turn malignant.

Remedy for the southeast: The solution to the problem here is water, which is an ideal cure for the afflictions caused by element disharmony. Use a water feature that has running or *yang* water. An aquarium is good but even a small fish bowl will help since water will exhaust the metal energy and simultaneously enhance the wood *chi*. So water is a must in the southeast in the year 2002.

☆ The Number 8

This number flies into the northwest, which is the only auspicious sector for the year 2002. This sector enjoys extremely good luck. Not only is the 8 intrinsically lucky but, in flying into the northwest, the earth energy of 8 produces the metal energy so good for the northwest. There is really no need to do anything except keep this sector of the house used at all times. Play music, open and close the doors, spend time here! The more this sector is used the more good luck will come into your home.

How to activate the northwest: A sure way to energize the northwest is to have a really proud image of *Kuan Kung*, the victorious general deified by the Chinese as the god of wealth. Try to find a *Kuan Kung* made of brass – which is heavy and solid and dripping with metal *chi*. It will be fantastic if you can place him in the northwest of your home. Since this is the only good sector of the home in 2002, make sure you make the most of it by activating it.

Metallic windchimes (an eight-rod one is best here) and golden coins will also be excellent. The placement of crystals in the northwest is also a great idea since crystals signify the earth, which produces metal.

☆ The Number 9

This number flies into the west, signifying fire flying into metal. This is a destructive relationship since fire destroys metal. Anyone with doors placed here or with rooms in the west part of their homes will definitely not have good luck. It is important to place remedies.

Remedy for the west: The best way to overcome the annual flying star affliction is to strengthen the metal energy with the earth element. This means using boulders, crystals, or porcelain urns. The earth energy will strengthen metal while exhausting the fire energy. Place quartz crystals or amethysts in the corner or, better yet, place lots of crystal gem trees here to simultaneously utilize auspicious symbolism as well.

The Monthly Charts of 2002

The year 2002 is made up of twelve months and the monthly stars of these twelve months are reproduced here. By referring to the monthly star numbers in conjunction with the annual numbers in each of the direction sectors (also known as palaces), it is possible to get an indication of the general luck of the different sectors during each month of the year.

The monthly and annual stars should be read in conjunction with the natal charts of houses to get a more accurate and detailed reading of the luck, prospects, and dangers facing different houses and their residents.

In fact, more important than checking for your good fortune is to find out how the warnings offered by the star analysis can be acted upon. In most circumstances there are excellent remedies that can overcome, or at least reduce, the effect of bad stars, although there are times when afflictions are so severe that it's hard to completely overcome their negative effect.

For 2002, however, although most of the grids are afflicted by one negative problem or other (except grid northwest which enjoys stunningly good fortune this year), for the most part the negative impact on house luck can be reduced and even completely overcome. This is due to the nature of the afflictions.

The monthly star numbers in the charts that follow are the smaller numbers indicated on the right-hand side of the large numbers. The large numbers in the center of each of the small squares are the annual numbers for the year. Both numbers must be considered in order to assess their overall impact.

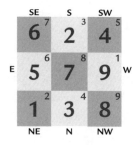

☆ FIRST MONTH February 4 to March 6

The Lo Shu number of the first month is 8, so the center number of the first month's star is 8.

The good luck sectors for the first month are the northwest, west, and southeast. In the northwest the annual 8 is magnified by the monthly

9 star, making a lucky situation even luckier. In the west, the annual number and month number add up to 10. The 1 star brings the luck of career and this is enhanced by the annual 9. In the southeast the annual 6 is strongly supported by the monthly lucky star 7.

The afflicted sectors in the first month are the southwest, where the monthly 5 yellow flies in; and the northeast, where the illness star 2 afflicts the sector. The south is also seriously hurt by the 3 star, which combines with the annual 2 star to bring problems associated with lawsuits and legal entanglements.

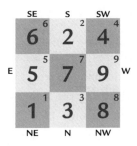

☆ SECOND MONTH March 6 to April 5

In the second month the northwest benefits from the double 8 star. This is because the Lo Shu number for the month is 7, similar to the year Lo Shu. Thus, in this second month, the fortunes of the year are strengthened. Those with rooms in the northwest or whose main door is located there should take advantage of the good combination of star numbers. For the same reason the sectors northeast, southeast, and southwest also have good stars.

The afflicted sectors are the east sector, which now has to cope with the double 5 yellow; and the south, which comes under the influence of the double 2, which brings illness. This should be a warning to those with rooms in these sectors. If the main door of your home is located in either the east or the south, you should be extra careful this month.

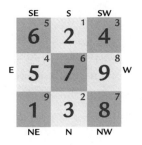

☆ THIRD MONTH April 5 to May 6

The third month indicates that the northwest continues to be lucky, as the month star does not hurt but, in fact, strengthens the element of that sector. Those of you enjoying the good luck of the northwest can look forward to continued good times. Other good sectors are the northeast, with numbers adding up to 10; and the west, where the month 8 flies in to enhance the sector.

The major affliction this month affects those with main doors or important rooms located in the north of their home. The 3/2 combination of numbers brings stresses arising from legal entanglements, strong arguments, and quarrels. It is vital to place an urn of *yin* (unmoving) water to cool down the sector. The monthly 5 in the southeast is kept under control.

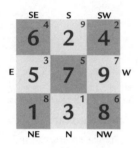

☆ FOURTH MONTH May 6 to June 6

In the fourth month the 5 yellow has flown to the center of the home. This creates the *chi* of illness for everyone – especially when combined with the 7, whose intrinsic negativity comes to light when activated by the 5. In the center, which is of the earth element, 5 becomes very strong. This is a month when everyone should be extra careful not to get sick. The west, the south, and the east are afflicted sectors. Do not make important decisions if your room is located in any of these sectors.

The northwest is strengthened by the 6 and continues to be very auspicious. So too is the northeast, where the month 8 also strengthens the luck of the sector. If your bedroom is located in either of these sectors, it spells good fortune this month. You can invest in the stock market and buy shares with confidence.

☆ FIFTH MONTH June 6 to July 7

In the fifth month, luck in the south vastly improves. The numbers add up to 10, making this sector suddenly very auspicious. Good news also comes to the southwest, where the 4/1 combination brings luck to those in love and those pursuing careers in the communications business.

The east, however, is very bad this month. The 5/2 combination makes it highly likely that anyone sleeping or working in this sector of their home or building will get seriously sick. If you are in this situation, either move out of the room for the month or hang a six-rod windchime in the room to overcome the strongly afflicted earth *chi* created by the number combination. These intangible negative forces are very strong. Certainly do not move furniture around, cut trees, or dig holes in the east sector this month. The effect can be instant illness (I tried doing this once just to test out this theory and lost my voice for a month!)

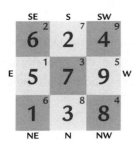

☆ SIXTH MONTH July 7 to August 8

In the sixth month, luck flies to the north and northeast sectors. In the north the monthly 8 brings good fortune and although it is very mild good fortune, it is a turn for the better after the stress of previous months. In the northeast the lucky 6 flies in to complement the 1, bringing good money luck to residents occupying that sector. A 6/1 combination spells good fortune.

The west, however, is seriously afflicted this month as the 5 yellow's negative impact is further strengthened by the annual 9. Illness and loss could befall residents occupying this sector. The same can be said of the south, where the 7 comes in to meet with the 2, although here the effect is nowhere as serious. Despite the fact that it can bring robbery and the luck of being cheated, since we are still in period 7, its negative impact is not as great.

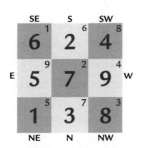

☆ SEVENTH MONTH August 8 to September 8

In the seventh month the lucky sectors are north, southeast, and northwest. The north enjoys the sum of 10 combination, which brings overriding good luck to everyone occupying the sector. In the southeast there is the powerfully auspicious *ho tu* combination of 6/1, bringing money and success luck to those occupying this sector. Also, the water element of 1 complements the wood *chi* of the sector thereby adding to the energy of the sector. The northwest has the *ho tu* combination of 8/3 and this brings good fortune in the areas of growth and progress.

The sector suffering from afflictions this month is the east, where the 5/9 combination brings illness, the potential for severe loss, and the possibility of accidents. Residents occupying the east should place water in the sector to control the 9 and enhance the wood element of the sector.

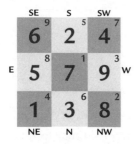

☆ EIGHTH MONTH September 8 to October 8

In the eighth month the best luck comes from the northwest, the northeast, and the southwest. The northwest enjoys the sum of 10 combination while the northeast has the 1/4 combination which brings auspicious love luck, as well as good energy for those in the writing professions. Scholars and those taking exams will do extremely well if they reside in this sector. The southwest, meanwhile, has the 4/7 combination, which also brings good fortune.

The south is extremely afflicted. Move out of there if possible since the 2/5 combine to bring severe sickness and the possibility of accidents.

Overall, however, the luck of the month favors investments and money luck.

☆ NINTH MONTH October 8 to November 7

In the ninth month good fortune visits those with rooms in the southeast. The auspicious 8 flies in to combine with the 6 annual star, bringing some money luck and the promise of some new venture. Those in the northwest also enjoy excellent good fortune. Residents in the southwest will benefit from the sum of 10 combination.

The east sector will experience some problems with young children (especially sons) this month. There is shouting and screaming, and disobedience is a problem. Move them out of that sector. The west also suffers from afflictions relating to young girls of the family. Take care they do not get involved with bad company this month. Again, moving them out of the afflicted sector could be helpful. Otherwise there could be some severe consequences. Overall this is a month to be careful.

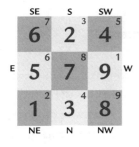

☆ TENTH MONTH November 7 to December 7

The tenth month overall is quite a lucky month; one in which the auspicious 8 flies into the center thereby spreading its positive influence. Lucky sectors are the west, which enjoys the sum of 10 combination; the northwest, where the 9 strengthens the annual 8 star; and the southeast, where 7 comes in to expand the influence of the annual 6.

The south, however, is seriously afflicted by the 2/3 combination. There will be lots of quarrels, fights, and misunderstandings within the home and with outsiders. Stay out of the south to avoid confrontational hostility wearing you down.

The 5 yellow in the southwest is very strong since the southwest is an earth sector. Hang six-rod windchimes to control the pernicious effect of the monthly 5. Otherwise there is a danger of fatal illness or scandals.

For more on the luck of the tenth month you can also refer to the luck of the first month as the star combinations are similar.

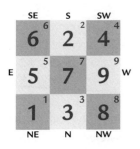

☆ ELEVENTH MONTH December 7 to January 6

In the eleventh month the northwest benefits from the double 8 star. This is because, as in the second month, the month Lo Shu is 7, similar to the year Lo Shu. Thus in this month the luck of the year is strengthened. Those with rooms in the northwest or whose main door is located there should take advantage of the good combination of star numbers. For the same reason the northeast, southeast, and southwest sectors also have good stars.

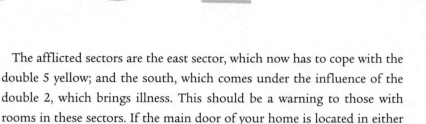

The afflicted sectors are the east sector, which now has to cope with the double 5 yellow; and the south, which comes under the influence of the double 2, which brings illness. This should be a warning to those with rooms in these sectors. If the main door of your home is located in either the east or the south, you should be extra careful this month.

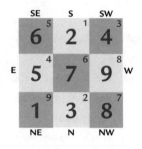

SE ⁵	S ¹	SW ³
6	**2**	**4**
E ⁴	⁶	⁸ W
5	**7**	**9**
⁹	²	⁷
1	**3**	**8**
NE	N	NW

☆ TWELFTH MONTH January 6 to February 4

The twelfth month indicates that the northwest continues to be lucky, as the month star does not hurt the sector but in fact strengthens the element of that sector. Those of you enjoying the good luck of northwest can look forward to continued good times as the year draws to a close. Other good sectors are the northeast, with numbers adding up to 10; and the west, where the month 8 flies in to enhance the sector.

The major affliction this month affects those with main doors or important rooms located in the north of their home. The 3/2 combination of numbers bring stresses arising from legal entanglements and quarrels. It is vital to place an urn of *yin* (unmoving) water to cool down the sector. The monthly 5 in the southeast is kept under control. Romance luck of the southwest, however, will be marred by quarrels and misunderstandings.

Use the twelve monthly *Lo Shu* flying star charts to track the luck of the year. If you study the numbers and their meanings (covered in the earlier section of Part One) you will soon develop a feel for their preliminary meanings and become adept in interpreting flying star charts. In all the different charts the meanings of the numbers and the combination of numbers is the same.

Once you master the meanings of the numbers, you will be ready to proceed. If you wish, you can also examine the *yin* and *yang* characteristics of numbers and also recall their elements. To obtain matching elements always go back to the original *Lo Shu* square and *Pa Kua* arrangement of the Later Heaven trigrams (see page 48).

Use the analysis given of the 16 different houses in Part Two to practice, and to discover the luck of different houses at the same time. This book then becomes an excellent way for you to gain familiarity with Flying Star feng shui – a very advanced system of feng shui analysis favored by almost all the authentic masters of China, Taiwan, and Hong Kong.

DETAILED HOUSE ANALYSIS

Method 1 –
8 Houses Based
on their Sitting Trigrams

2002

The Trigram of Houses

There are two methods of investigating the feng shui luck of houses in any given year. One is simple, the other a little more complex. We will begin with the simple method, which examines the luck of houses based on what is referred to as their sitting trigrams. This method classifies all homes and buildings into eight types based on the eight trigrams around the *Pa Kua*.

The eight trigrams around the *Pa Kua* are based on what is known as the Later Heaven arrangement of the trigrams. This means that each trigram is allotted a direction according to the sequence of trigram arrangement shown in the *yang Pa Kua*. This is shown in the illustration here. From the illustration note the names of the trigrams, as well as the *Lo Shu* number of the trigrams as follows. When your house is sitting in the:

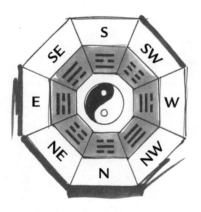

☆ North – it is a *KAN* house, with the *Lo Shu* number 1

☆ South – it is a *LI* house, with the *Lo Shu* number 9

☆ East – it is a *CHEN* house, with the *Lo Shu* number 3

☆ West – it is a *TUI* house, with the *Lo Shu* number 7

☆ Southeast – it is a *SUN* house, with the *Lo Shu* number 4

☆ Southwest – it is a *KUN* house, with the *Lo Shu* number 2

☆ Northeast – it is a *KEN* house, with the *Lo Shu* number 8

☆ Northwest – it is a *CHIEN* house, with the *Lo Shu* number 6

Taking Compass Readings

To determine what kind of trigram house yours is, you must learn to use a compass to take directions. Invest in a good compass – one that is reliable and accurate, and has the degrees marked out clearly. Make sure to take accurate readings from the compass. In fact, for feng shui purposes, it is a good idea to take at least three readings for accuracy. Please note that readings should be taken at the main door, standing inside and facing squarely outside. This direction is known as the facing direction of the house.

Once you know the facing direction of your house you will be able to determine its sitting direction. This is the direct opposite of the facing direction. So when the house faces north it is said to be sitting south and will therefore be a *Li* house. When a house faces east it is said to be sitting west and is a *Tui* house, and so forth.

Each trigram house is said to have its own reigning *Lo Shu* number, and from this number the feng shui chart of the house can be generated based on the flight sequence of the star numbers according to the original *Lo Shu* square.

TRIGRAM house	Facing direction	Sitting direction
A *LI* house	is facing north	is sitting south
A *KAN* house	is facing south	is sitting north
A *CHEN* house	is facing west	is sitting east
A *TUI* house	is facing east	is sitting west
A *KUN* house	is facing northeast	is sitting southwest
A *CHIEN* house	is facing southeast	is sitting northwest
A *KEN* house	is facing southwest	is sitting northeast
A *SUN* house	is facing northwest	is sitting southeast

To assess the luck of the different sectors of the house we combine the numbers of the 2002 feng shui chart, which has 7 as the center number, with the trigram chart of the house. This generates a special chart which shows two numbers in each grid of the *Lo Shu* square.

The center number is the number of the house grids based on its reigning *Lo Shu* number; the smaller number is the number of the annual stars (see pages 61 – 71). The luck of each sector is then read in accordance with the meanings associated with the combination of the two numbers. To enable the reader to follow the analysis of each of the eight houses in 2002, the following table sets out the meanings of the combination of the trigram and annual numbers. This is a very valuable table and learning the meanings of these numbers will go a long way toward bringing you success in your feng shui practice.

The Meanings of Trigram and Annual Number Combinations

The trigram number	The annual number	Indicated divinations and outcomes of the combination	Enhancers for good luck combinations or remedies for bad luck combinations
1	1	Excellent for academic studies, research, and creative work. Good money luck. If afflicted by month star 5 or 2, there could be kidney-related illness. Accidents caused by excessive drinking and alcohol problems	To enhance and also to control affliction, use six-rod windchimes
1	2	There could be marriage problems and a danger of loss of a child through miscarriage. Beware of car accidents	Use plants to exhaust the water number 1 and strengthen the earth element
1	3	Heartache caused by gossip and slander. There could be lawsuits and legal entanglements	Use water and water plants to enhance
1	4	Political luck. Media and publicity luck. Romance luck, especially for women. Good writing luck for authors	Use slow-moving water but not too much

The trigram number	The annual number	Indicated divinations and outcomes of the combination	Enhancers for good luck combinations or remedies for bad luck combinations
1	5	Health problems – sicknesses, food poisonings. Injury caused by accidents	Use a windchime
1	6	Excellent career luck. Promotion. Good money luck. Headaches, especially when month 5 or 2 comes in	Enhance with metal
1	7	Good money luck in period of 7, but it is also an indication that there will be cut-throat competition	Enhance with crystals or gem tree
1	8	Excellent wealth luck. There could be misunderstandings between loved ones, siblings, and good friends. Business partners have problems	Enhance with crystals
1	9	Good for both career and money luck, but can turn bad when 5 flies in. Eye problems	Do not enhance
2	1	Stress develops in the marriage. Danger of miscarriage, accidents, and loss of a loved one	Use windchimes to control the bad star 2
2	2	Not a good indication. Magnifies strong negative feelings. Illness and accidents possible	Six-rod windchimes
2	3	Arguments and misunderstandings of the most severe kind. Back-stabbing, hatred, legal disputes	Use still water to cool tempers. Do not disturb
2	4	Wives and mothers-in-law quarrel and fight. Disharmony. Good indications for writers and those in journalism. Good for those at school	Use water

The trigram number	The annual number	Indicated divinations and outcomes of the combination	Enhancers for good luck combinations or remedies for bad luck combinations
2	5	Extremely inauspicious. Total loss and catastrophe. This is one of the most dangerous combinations in Flying Star technology, and when the 5 flies in, anyone staying here can suddenly develop terminal illness	Use strong windchimes (plenty). Beware, do not have fire – could result in death
2	6	Very easy life of ease and leisure, power and authority. This auspicious combination is spoilt if a five-rod windchime is placed here. The trinity (*tien ti ren*) gets activated in a negative way	Do not use windchimes. If there is sickness related to the stomach, place a red amulet here
2	7	There is money during the period of 7 but luck of children will not be good. Problems conceiving children. Unscrupulous people at work against you	Use metal (bells) and metal windchimes. Also hang sword of coins
2	8	Richness and wealth but there is ill health, although this is minor and can be remedied	Use water to overcome bad health star
2	9	Extreme bad luck. Nothing succeeds unless remedied. Not a good indication for children	Use water plants. Also use coins or a windchime
3	1	Heartache caused by gossip and slander. There could be lawsuits and legal entanglements	Use water to enhance and water plants
3	2	Dangerous for those in politics – lawsuits, even jail. Gossip, slander. Bad luck for women, obesity	Some masters recommend gold and fire
3	3	Gossip and slander. Quarrels. Robbery possible	Use sword of coins

The trigram number	The annual number	Indicated divinations and outcomes of the combination	Enhancers for good luck combinations or remedies for bad luck combinations
3	4	Heartache caused by sexual scandal	Use bright lights
3	5	Loss of wealth. Severe cash flow problems. If a bedroom is here, financial loss is severe. If the kitchen is here, sickness is inevitable. Do not stay here	Exhaust the 5 with copper mountain painting
3	6	Time of slow growth. Leg injuries. Bad for young males	Use yin (still) water
3	7	Robbery or burglary. Violence. Possibility of injury from knives or guns. Blood	Use water
3	8	Not good for children under 12 years. Danger to limbs	Use bright lights to cure
3	9	Robbery encounter. Lawsuits. Fights	Use yin (still) water
☒ 4	1	Very good romance luck but too much water leads to sex scandals. Affairs lead to unhappiness and breakup of family. Excellent creative and writing luck	Kuan Yin statue or image of laughing Buddha for some divine help
4	2	Illness of internal organs. Husband has affairs	Use amethysts
4	3	Emotional stress due to relationship and sex problems	Use red to overcome
☒ 4	4	Excellent for writing and creative luck. Very attractive to opposite sex. Romance will flourish	Fresh flowers to enhance growth of romance
4	5	Sexually transmitted skin diseases. Breast cancer	Use painting of water and mountain as cure

The trigram number	The annual number	Indicated divinations and outcomes of the combination	Enhancers for good luck combinations or remedies for bad luck combinations
4	6	Money luck, but creativity dries up. Bad luck indicated for women, especially pregnant women	Strengthen earth element with crystals
4	7	Bad luck in love. Will get cheated on by opposite sex. Sickness of the thighs and lower abdomen	Use water to control
4	8	Excellent career luck for writers. Bad for very young children. Injury to limbs indicated	Use lights to combat
4	9	A time for preparation. Good for students. Need to be careful of fire breaking out	Use wood or plants
5	1	Hearing problems and also sex-related illness	Use a windchime
5	2	Misfortunes and extreme bad luck. Illness may be fatal	Use a windchime etc.
5	3	Money troubles. Disputes. Bad business luck	Use coins
5	4	Creativity dries up. Sickness. Skin problems	Use water/painting of a mountain
5	5	A very critical combination. Extreme danger indicated. Serious illness and accidents that can be fatal. Take care	Use metal six-rod windchimes to overcome
5	6	Bad financial luck. Loss. Diseases related to the head region. Danger also to the man	Place 6 coins under the carpet
5	7	Arguments abound. Mouth-related illness	Use coins and bells

The trigram number	The annual number	Indicated divinations and outcomes of the combination	Enhancers for good luck combinations or remedies for bad luck combinations
5	8	Problems related to the limbs, joints, and bones of the body. It is necessary to be wary of rough sports	Use water to pacify
5	9	Bad luck all round. Do not speculate or gamble as you are sure to lose. Eye problems. Danger of fire	Use water
6	1	Financial luck and high achievers in the family. Headaches through excessive stress	Enhance with metal
6	2	Great affluence and everything successful. Stomach problems. Patriarch could suffer sickness	No need to enhance but control with bells
6	3	Unexpected windfall. Speculative luck. Possible leg injury	Enhance with gemstones
6	4	Unexpected windfall for women of the family. Lower body injury. Pregnant women should be careful	Enhance with crystals
6	5	Money luck blocked. Sickness could prevail	Use bells
6	6	Excellent money luck from heaven but too much metal can be dangerous, so do not enhance with metal	No need to enhance
6	7	Competitive squabbling over money. Arguments	Use water to curb
6	8	Wealth, popularity, prosperity. Great richness. Probably the best combination in Flying Star technique. Those in love are in for a lonely period	Enhance with water and make sure you have an entrance or window in that sector

The trigram number	The annual number	Indicated divinations and outcomes of the combination	Enhancers for good luck combinations or remedies for bad luck combinations
6	9	Money luck. Frustration between generations leading to arguments between young and old	Use water to reduce the friction
7	1	Extremely good prosperity luck. Competition is deadly	Use water feature
7	2	Money luck dissipates. Children luck is dimmed	Use windchimes
7	3	Grave danger of injury to limbs. Be careful	Use water
7	4	Taken for a ride by someone of the opposite sex. Pregnant women should take care	Use water
7	5	Problems caused by excessive gossiping. Danger of poisoning or anything to do with the mouth	Use metal coins, bells, or windchimes
7	6	Negative *chi* – "sword fighting killing breath"	Use water
7	7	Victory over the competition. Money luck. Sex life gets a boost for young people. Beware of over- indulgence	Use water to curb excesses
7	8	Same as above but better	Use water
7	9	All troubles are caused through vulnerability to sexual advances. There is danger of fire	Use earth (big boulders) to press down bad luck
8	1	Excellent and auspicious prosperity luck. Career advancement. Money luck, but sibling rivalry prevails	Enhance with water

The trigram number	The annual number	Indicated divinations and outcomes of the combination	Enhancers for good luck combinations or remedies for bad luck combinations
8	2	Wealth creation possible. Properties and asset accumulation but danger of illness	Use mountain principle. Boulder tied with red thread
8	3	Move children away from this sector. Limb injuries	Use red, yellow
8	4	Overpowering matriarch. Love lives of younger generation suffer from mother problems. Limb injuries	Use fire, or red to overcome
8	5	Problems related to the limbs, joints, and bones of the body. It is necessary to be wary of rough sports	Use water to pacify
8	6	Wealth, popularity, prosperity. Great richness. One of the best combinations in Flying Star system, though love life goes through a rough patch	Enhance with crystals make sure entrance or window in that sector
8	7	Prevail over the competition. Money luck. Sex life gets a boost for young people. Beware over-indulgence.	Use water to curb excesses
8	8	Excellent wealth creation luck. Very favorable.	No need to enhance
8	9	Excellent for money and celebration but misunderstandings between the younger and older generations can turn nasty	Use water to calm the fire
9	1	Good for both career and money luck, but can turn bad when 5 flies in. Eye problems	Do not enhance

The trigram number	The annual number	Indicated divinations and outcomes of the combination	Enhancers for good luck combinations or remedies for bad luck combinations
9	2	Extremely bad luck. Nothing succeeds unless remedied. Not a good indication for children	Use water plants. Also use coins or a windchime
9	3	Robbery encounter. Lawsuits. Fights. Fire hazard	Use yin (still) water
9	4	A time for preparation. Good for students. Be careful of fire	Use wood or plants
9	5	Bad luck all round. Do not speculate or gamble as you are sure to lose. Eye problems. Danger of fire	Use water
9	6	Money luck. Frustration between generations leading to arguments between young and old	Use water to reduce the friction
9	7	Troubles caused through vulnerability to sexual advances. There is danger of fire	Use earth (big boulders) to press down bad luck
9	8	Excellent for money and celebration but misunderstandings between the younger and older generations can turn nasty	Use water to calm the fire
9	9	Good or bad depending on other indications	Do not enhance

The grid illustrations in this section show the main door of the house at the top. This should make it easier for you to superimpose the nine sector grid on top of a layout plan of your home and thus match the luck analysis to each of the rooms in your home. Please determine which trigram your home belongs to and then read the analysis accordingly. Those living in apartments please use the facing direction of the whole building to determine the trigram of your whole building. This is the chart to superimpose on your apartment layout plan to analyze the luck of your apartment. Remember to always match the sectors according to the compass.

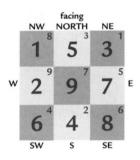

1 The Luck Analysis of a Li House

A *Li* house faces north and sits south. So this house faces between 337.5 degrees to 22.5 degrees on the compass, a total of 45 degrees. Exact north is 0 degrees. Look at the chart here and note that the big number is the trigram number with the trigram's *Lo Shu* number 9 in the center, while the small number to the side is the annual number, with 7 in the center. The lucky sectors are starred.

NW 1/8 Combination ☆
There is excellent wealth luck for residents living in this part of the home. The luck can be further enhanced with crystals. However, misunderstandings between loved ones, siblings, and good friends can arise due to the influence of the 1 water number. Business partners could develop problems but these should blow over since prospects for income growth are excellent this year.

W 2/9 Combination
This sector suffers from extreme bad luck. Nothing succeeds unless remedies are used. This is also not a good corner for your children to have their rooms, as the indications suggest they could get sick frequently. Use water plants in this corner. Also use coins or windchimes.

SW 6/4 Combination

The southwest brings an unexpected windfall for the women of the family. If they are residing in this part of the home it is even better. The negatives indicated are problems associated with the lower body. The lower limbs and buttock areas could suffer some injury. Pregnant women should be very careful. Enhance the sector with crystals.

S 4/2 Combination

Those staying in the south of the house could develop problems associated with the internal organs. Make sure there is no water on the right-hand side of the front door as the indication is that the husband of the home could be susceptible to starting an illicit love affair. To calm this, place an amethyst under the bed.

SE 8/6 Combination ☆

Wealth, popularity, prosperity – great richness. One of the best combinations in the Flying Star system. All this is found in your southeast sector this year if this is your house. Your love life, however, goes through a rough patch. Enhance with hanging crystals by the window to catch the sun's magical rays in the morning. Make sure there is an entrance or window in this sector.

E 7/5 Combination

Problems caused by excessive gossiping. Danger of poisoning or anything to do with the mouth. Use metal coins and windchimes.

NE 3/1 Combination

Heartache caused by gossip and slander. There could be lawsuits and legal entanglements. Use water and water plants.

N 5/3 Combination
Money troubles. Disputes. Bad business luck. Use coins.

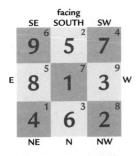

	facing	
SE	SOUTH	SW
9 ⁶	5 ²	7 ⁴
E 8 ⁵	1 ⁷	3 ⁹ W
4 ¹	6 ³	2 ⁸
NE	N	NW

2 The Luck Analysis of a Kan House

A *Kan* house faces south and sits north. So this house faces between 157.5 degrees to 202.5 degrees on the compass, a total of 45 degrees. Exact south is 180 degrees. Look at the chart here and note that the big number is the trigram number with the trigram's *Lo Shu* number 1 in the center, while the small number to the side is the annual number with 7 in the center. The lucky sectors are starred.

SE 9/6 Combination

There is money luck for those staying in this corner of the house but there are also real problems arising from frustration between the generations. This leads to arguments between the young people and the more elderly people living in the home. Watch out for this and place *yin* (still) water to reduce the friction. Use water that has been energized by the moonlight.

E 8/5 Combination

There are problems relating to the limbs, joints, and bones of the body for those staying in the east sector of this house. It is necessary to be wary of rough sports. Older people should not bathe at night. Water in the east will strengthen the energy here.

NE 4/1 Combination ☆

The northeast of this house has very good romance luck. Those who are in love will be very happy but they must not forget that too much water in this corner could lead to sex scandals and problems. There might be extramarital affairs leading to unhappiness and the breakup of family. However, there is also excellent creative and writing luck so writers living in this part of an apartment block or house will enjoy a rise in fortunes.

N 6/3 Combination

Those in the north, i.e. living at the back of the house, will enjoy an unexpected windfall, usually of a monetary nature – perhaps a fat bonus!

There is also excellent speculative luck. On the negative side there is danger of leg injury. Gemstones will bring enhanced good luck. Those who gamble should wear diamonds and jade during the year of the water horse to activate the luck.

NW 2/8 Combination ☆

Richness and wealth are indicated in the northwest corner. Most people living in the northwest of their buildings and homes will enjoy very good fortune this year. There is the specter of ill health, although this is minor and can be remedied. *Yang* (bubbling) water will overcome the bad health star.

W 3/9 Combination

People staying in the west part of the home could have an unfortunate encounter with robbers. There might also be lawsuits, and serious arguments leading to fights that can turn nasty. Use *yin* (still) water.

SW 7/4 Combination

You could be taken for a ride by someone of the opposite sex. Pregnant women should take care.

S 5/2 Combination

Very very bad. Misfortunes and extreme bad luck. Illness may be fatal. Hang 6 metal windchimes.

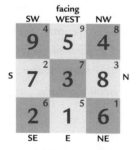

3 The Luck Analysis of a Chen House

A *Chen* house faces west and sits east. So this house faces between 247.5 degrees to 292.5 degrees on the compass, a total of 45 degrees. Exact west is 270 degrees. Look at the chart here and note that the big number is the trigram number with the trigram's *Lo Shu* number 3 in the center, while the small number to the side is the annual number with 7 in the center. The lucky sectors are starred.

SW 9/4 Combination

A time for preparation. This is intrinsically a lucky sector which has been enhanced by the creative 4 star number. So rooms here are good for students and writers. Those in love will also enjoy good luck here. Be careful of fire though – some water energy here might be a good idea.

S 7/2 Combination

Money luck evaporates in the south sector this year. It is also not a good time for children. Those sleeping here will tend to get sick and feel irritable throughout the year. It's a good idea to use another room.

SE 2/6 Combination

The numbers indicate a very easy life of leisure this year for those occupying this room. There is also power and authority. This auspicious combination is spoilt if a five-rod windchime is placed here. The trinity (*tien ti ren*) gets activated in a negative way. Do not use windchimes. If there is sickness related to the stomach, place a red amulet here.

E 1/5 Combination

People in this sector will be assailed by health problems. There is frequent sickness afflicting all members of the family but more those who live in this part of the home. If the family room is here, the health afflictions affect everyone. There is food poisoning and injury caused by accidents. Move into another room if possible.

NE 6/1 Combination ☆

A very lucky corner. There is financial luck in this corner and those staying here will emerge as the high achievers in the family. There are headaches, however, which are caused by excessive stress.

N 8/3 Combination

Move children away from this sector. The numbers indicate some kind of minor injury to the limbs. Correct with amulets painted in red on yellow paper.

NW 4/8 Combination ☆

There is excellent career luck for writers but this sector is not good for children, especially those under 12 years. Injury to limbs is indicated. Use lights to combat this affliction – perhaps a red lamp kept on for about three hours each night.

W 5/9 Combination

The luck of this sector is very bad. The 5/9 combination can only be controlled by a six-rod windchime which ideally has the *Pa Kua* coin suspended from it. If you cannot find such a windchime, then use a normal metallic six-rod windchime. If this does not completely overcome the bad luck of this sector, use six of these chimes and augment further with six coins under the carpet. If the main door is placed in this part of the house you should move it a little to the right, if at all possible, so it goes into the northwest sector which is so lucky this year. Remember that 2002 is generally not a good year and that the northwest is just about the only all round auspicious corner for everyone, so if you can tap into it for your door it will be great. Moving the door to the northwest does not mean the door has to change direction. It can still face north if you so wish.

4 The Luck Analysis of a TUI House

A *Tui* house faces east and sits west. So this house faces between 67.5 degrees to 112.5 degrees on the compass, a total of 45 degrees. Exact east is 90 degrees. Look at the chart here and note that the big number is the trigram number with the trigram's *Lo Shu* number 7 in the center, while the small number to the side is the annual number with 7 in the center. The lucky sectors are starred.

NE 1/1 Combination ☆

This is an excellent sector for academic studies, research, and creative work. Put your kids here if they are still at school. Even if they are at boarding school, the good feng shui of their room will benefit them. This sector also has good money luck. If afflicted by month star 5 or 2, there could be kidney-related illness, accidents caused by excessive drinking, and alcoholic problems. Generally a good sector though.

N 3/3 Combination

If you have your room here at home or at work, i.e. in the north of a *Tui* building, then you will become the victim of gossip and slander. Office politics could defeat you. Hang a coin sword tied with red thread on your right of your work desk. There will definitely be quarrels, and you could also get robbed.

NW 8/8 Combination ☆

Excellent wealth creation luck. Very favourable. Everything goes right. Nothing goes wrong!

W 9/9 Combination

Usually 9/9 depends on other indications to define its luck. Here, fire enters the west thereby burning the *chi* of metal. The effect is negative for this room. Use water to overcome.

SW 4/4 Combination ☆

These numbers bring excellent writing and creative luck for residents. Those staying here will also enjoy the chi which makes them very attractive to the opposite sex. Romance will flourish. Fresh flowers are excellent as they will magnify the growth energy of romance.

S 2/2 Combination

Not a good indication. Magnifies strong negative feelings. Illness and accidents are possible.

SE 6/6 Combination ☆

Excellent money luck from heaven, but too much metal can be dangerous – especially in a wood sector. Do not enhance with metal. This will make the *chi* too oppressive.

E 5/5 Combination

A very critical combination. Extreme danger is indicated – serious illness and accidents that can be fatal. Take care whenever you leave the house. Do not go out too late at nights. Keep a low profile.

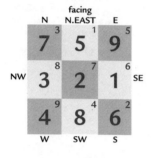

5 The Luck Analysis of a Kun House

A *Kun* house faces northeast and sits southwest. So this house faces between 22.5 degrees to 67.5 degrees on the compass, a total of 45 degrees. Exact northeast is 45 degrees. Look at the chart here and note that the big number is the trigram number with the trigram's *Lo Shu* number 2 in the center, while the small number to the side is the annual number with 7 in the center. The lucky sectors are starred.

N 7/3 Combination

The numbers in the north indicate grave danger of injury to limbs for residents here, so there is a need to be very careful. Use water to strengthen the sector.

NW 3/8 Combination

This sector is not good for children under 12 years. There is some danger to limbs indicated by the combination of numbers. To overcome this affliction use bright lights to strengthen the auspicious 8.

W 4/9 Combination

This combination of numbers suggests a time for preparation so the sector is good for students, although anyone engaged in studies will benefit from staying in this part of the house. There is a danger of fire breaking out in this sector so be careful. Use plants to enhance the trigram number of the house.

SW 8/4 Combination

The problem here is the extremely strong and overpowering matriarchal energy. The love lives of the younger generation could suffer from mother or mother-in-law problems.

S 6/2 Combination ☆

Great affluence and everything is successful. This is an auspicious sector for anyone in business or wanting to climb the career ladder. Stomach problems. Patriarch could suffer sickness.

SE 1/6 Combination

Excellent career luck is indicated in this corner. If your room is here you could have a meaningful promotion at work. There is also good money luck. However, there is also the possibility of headaches, especially when the monthly 5 or 2 comes in.

E 9/5 Combination

Oh dear – the east suffers from bad luck all round. Do not speculate or gamble as you are sure to lose. There could be eye problems. Danger is posed by fire.

NE 5/1 Combination

The numbers are not promising. There are hearing problems and also sex-related illness. Place windchimes to overcome the problem caused by the 5 in the combination.

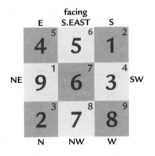

6 The Luck Analysis of a Chien House

A *Chien* house faces southeast and sits northwest. So this house faces between 112.5 degrees to 157.5 degrees on the compass, a total of 45 degrees. Exact southeast is 135 degrees. Look at the chart here and note that the big number is the trigram number with the trigram's *Lo Shu* number 6 in the center, while the small number to the side is the annual number with 7 in the center. The lucky sectors are starred.

E 4/5 Combination

The combination of numbers here this year is really quite unfortunate. They suggest the possibility of sexually transmitted illness, skin disease, and even heartaches. There is also the possibility of breast cancer. The remedy if your room is here is to use the "water and mountain" cure – place a painting of a mountain and water scene in your room.

NE 9/1 Combination ☆

This combination is good for both career and money luck, but it can turn bad easily when the monthly 5 flies in (check the monthly charts in the previous section). When that happens there is a possibility of severe eye infection. Generally, however, this is a lucky sector.

N 2/3 Combination

The numbers are suggestive of arguments and misunderstandings of the most severe kind – backstabbing, hatred, legal disputes. It is important not to have too much noise in this corner. Do not play loud music and do not hang windchimes here. Keep this place quiet.

NW 7/8 Combination ☆

A lucky sector. Anyone staying in this sector will prevail over their competition. There is money luck and relationship luck. Sex life gets a boost for young people. Just beware of overindulgence.

W 8/9 Combination ☆

Another good sector this year. Excellent for money and celebration. Materially there is little to complain about but there are problems in the family between younger and older members. These misunderstandings could turn nasty so be patient. Use *yin* (still) water to calm the fire.

SW 3/4 Combination

An afflicted love sector for this year. Love turns rough and sad. There is heartache caused by sexual scandal, betrayal, and infidelity. A good cure is to keep the place well lit with bright lights. Another excellent cure is to place crystals (amethyst geodes) under the bed.

S 1/2 Combination

An afflicted sector this year. There could be marriage problems and a danger of loss of a child through miscarriage. Beware of car accidents. Keep this corner quiet and place a *Pi yao* (the powerful creature of good fortune) here.

SE 5/6 Combination

Bad luck will cause financial loss. Diseases related to the head region are indicated, and danger to the patriarch. Place six coins under the carpet.

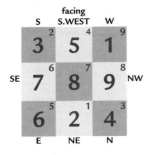

7 The Luck Analysis of a Ken House

A *Ken* house faces southwest and sits northeast. So this house faces between 202.5 degrees to 247.5 degrees on the compass, a total of 45 degrees. Exact southwest is 225 degrees. Look at the chart here and note that the big number is the trigram number with the trigram's *Lo Shu* number 8 in the center, while the small number to the side is the annual number with 7 in the center. The lucky sectors are starred.

S 3/2 Combination

The south of a *Ken* house takes on dangerous attributes for those who are in politics or in a high-profile situation. There could be lawsuits that can lead to serious consequences. Gossip, slander, and general bad luck affect women – who will also tend to suffer from obesity. Not a good sector so get out of there! Some masters recommend gold and fire to cleanse this sector's afflictions, but whatever you do keep the sector quiet.

SE 7/6 Combination

The southeast also has hostile *chi*. Here the affliction is called "sword fighting killing breath." Stay low key.

E 6/5 Combination

The east has its money and wealth luck blocked by the year star 5. It is annoying indeed since there is also the real possibility of illness dragging on. Sickness could prevail throughout the year.

NE 2/1 Combination

If your master bedroom is in this part of the house, stress develops in the marriage. There is also the danger of miscarriage, accidents, and loss of a loved one. This appears to be a fierce combination for the year and I recommend moving out of here at least temporarily. When the monthly 2 and 5 fly in the danger becomes most acute.

N 4/3 Combination

There is great emotional stress due to relationship and sex problems. Use red or fire energy to overcome this. Place a bright lamp in this corner of the home and keep it lit.

NW 9/8 Combination ☆

Excellent for money and celebration. The 8 of the year is enhanced by the trigram number in this sector. You can invest with some confidence and business will succeed, despite overall problems in the marketplace. The negative side is that misunderstandings between the younger and older generations will develop and could turn nasty. Use water to calm the fire. *Yin* (still) water that has stood for a few hours bathing in the light of a full moon will be best.

W 1/9 Combination ☆

The west sector indicates good luck for both career and money aspirations. Materially, it will be a successful year ahead. Danger comes only when the monthly 5 and 2 fly in – when they do, hang metal windchimes. Check the month charts to see when the 5 flies into the west. That is when things turn particularly bad. Eye problems are indicated, so be careful with sports such as swimming in those months.

SW 5/4 Combination
The southwest is afflicted and creativity simply dries up. There could be some sickness and skin problems. Use the "water and mountain cure" to totally obliterate these problems: hang a painting of mountains and water. Alternatively place a large crystal geode and an urn of water in this corner.

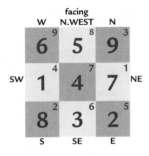

8 The Luck Analysis of a Sun House

A *Sun* house faces northwest and sits southeast. So this house faces between 292.5 degrees to 337.5 degrees on the compass, a total of 45 degrees. Exact northwest is 315 degrees. Look at the chart here and note that the big number is the trigram number with the trigram's *Lo Shu* number 4 in the center, while the small number to the side is the annual number with 7 in the center. The lucky sectors are starred.

W 6/9 Combination
This part of a *Sun* house will enjoy auspicious money luck during the year. Problems will arise only when the monthly 5 or 2 flies into the sector (check the monthly charts). There is also some frustration between the generations, leading to arguments between young and old.

SW 1/4 Combination ☆
This is a sector which enjoys excellent relationship and love luck. Those in politics will benefit from good media coverage and there is also excellent publicity luck. Romance luck, especially for women, is quite powerful this year if your room is located here. Finally, there is good writing luck for authors.

S 8/2 Combination ☆
Those residing here will benefit from the luck of wealth creation. Property and asset accumulation will occur and residents will also have the support of the Grand Duke Jupiter in this sector. There are some small illness afflictions but these are minor.

SE 3/6 Combination

Those staying in this sector will experience slow progress as there is little growth energy. When the 2 and 5 stars fly in, leg injuries could occur. It is a bad sector for young males.

E 2/5 Combination

Extremely inauspicious. Total loss and catastrophe. This is one of the most dangerous combinations in Flying Star technology, and when the monthly 5 flies in, anyone staying here can suddenly develop a terminal illness. Place windchimes in this corner and also use bells frequently to cleanse the space of this horrible energy. If you can, keep it unoccupied throughout the year.

NE 7/1 Combination ☆

Extremely good prosperity luck, although the competition facing those residing here is quite deadly. Nevertheless you will prevail. To make more sure of this it is an excellent idea to use an energizer such as a wonderful aquarium filled with goldfish. This signifies abundance. Water will also strengthen the annual lucky star which has flown into the sector. So use this star by activating it.

N 9/3 Combination

An afflicted sector. There is danger of a robbery encounter, lawsuits, fights, and fire. Use *yin* (still) water to overcome the danger.

NW 5/8 Combination

Residents here could suffer from problems related to the limbs, joints, and bones of the body. It is necessary to be wary of rough sports.

PART THREE

DETAILED HOUSE ANALYSIS

Method 2 –
Using the Flying Star Method

2002

The Flying Star Method

In this section we will analyze the luck of houses based on the Flying Star method of Feng Shui. This is a more complex method than the previous one, but it is the system used by all the practicing feng shui masters of Hong Kong, Taiwan, and China, and is the authentic method of calculating the changing luck of houses from year to year and from period to period.

We will analyze all sixteen natal charts of houses built or renovated during the current period of 7. These houses (which include office and apartment buildings as well) are said to be "period of 7" houses. This means that the natal charts presented in this section of the book are applicable to all houses and buildings that were constructed during the period of 7. Based on the Chinese *Hsia* calendar, the period of 7 started on February 4, 1984 and will end on February 4, 2004.

These charts also apply to all houses and buildings that have been renovated during the period of 7. There is a certain amount of controversy surrounding what actually constitutes a renovation. Some masters apply the criteria strictly and insist that unless the roof is changed or there has been massive knocking and banging, it does not constitute a renovation, and therefore does not qualify the house for a change of period. Other masters say that merely repainting the house would be considered as a renovation. Some feng shui masters even go so far as to insist that the period of the house for any residents is based on when the family moved into the home.

Based on personal experience and research, my view is that the house changes period when there is banging and knocking in the house. As for the "roof change" requirement, this can be a symbolic removal of a small part of the roof and then replacing it again. Taking this interpretation of the classical texts on Flying Star, I have come to the conclusion that well over 90 percent of most homes would qualify to be period of 7 homes. As such I am confining the luck analysis for 2002 to such houses and buildings.

Determining your House Chart

Once again, to determine your house chart, you must use a reliable and accurate compass that has the degrees marked out clearly. Make sure you know how to take readings from the compass. For Flying Star feng shui purposes you should take your readings standing square and placing your compass level with your tummy. The more detailed the reading the better. Please note when taking a reading that it must be taken at the main door, standing inside and facing out. Take the reading three times for accuracy. If electrical products are disturbing the compass, remove them first before taking the reading again.

In Flying Star feng shui, the direction which the house or building faces is the vital key to creating or calculating its natal chart. The formula for Flying Star is highly complex and difficult and is beyond the scope of this book. Instead, I have pre calculated the natal charts of all period 7 houses.

Emphasis is placed on analysis of good and bad luck for 2002 in these houses and on the suitable remedies which can reduce identified bad luck, rather than on the technique of generating the actual charts themselves. This approach makes Flying Star feng shui easy to apply and also instantly usable, even for total beginners.

The only things you need to do are the following:

☆ Check when your house was built or last renovated

☆ Invest in a good, reliable compass

☆ Take the direction which your main door faces

☆ If your main door does not face the main road but instead faces the garage, for instance, then you should use the orientation of the house to get your natal chart. In such an instance taking the direction is a little tricky. If you have another door – a secondary door or a sliding door – which faces the main road, use that door to take the orientation of the house

☆ Now check the direction against the table of directions on the following page to identify what kind of house yours is. The names of houses are expressed as directions. So a west 1 house is said to be facing west between 247.5 to 262.5 degrees. You can see why the accuracy of reading is essential when you realize that the direction your house faces determines what house it is – the natal chart changes depending on the facing direction.

Houses are named according to the door direction or orientation. The natal charts apply also to multi level buildings. The same natal chart will affect every floor level. The *Lo Shu* natal chart can be superimposed on every floor and the luck attributes of the nine palaces apply equally well at every level of the house. You can see that this method is different from the first method, which is a lot simpler. However, the Flying Star method offers a much more detailed reading of house luck for any year.

Taking the Direction of a Building

Consider the orientation of the building by determining where it is facing, as a whole. Consider the source of the most *yang* energy. This is usually the main road.

Consider most importantly where the main door is facing and use this as the orientation unless the main door is facing a garage or a wall completely away from the main road.

The center house in the series of sketches below has a door which faces the garage, so the orientation of this house is taken to be where the arrow is pointing – this is considered the general orientation of the house.

Main road – place of most yang energy

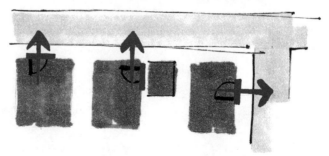

Identifying the House or Building

Once you have taken the facing direction at the main door of your house, you will be able to identify what kind of house or building yours is, in terms of its facing direction. This will allow you to identify the natal chart that applies to your house or building from the chart below. You can see that the degrees given require you to be quite exact when you take your compass reading. You will also notice that the Flying Star system splits each of the eight directions into three sub directions. Thus we have south 1, 2, and 3, and so forth. The natal charts for the second and third sub directions are the same, so there are a total of 16 natal charts to cover all the houses.

Orientation of building or direction of main door	The exact bearing in degrees read from the compass
SOUTH 1	157.5 to 172.5
SOUTH 2	172.5 to 187.5
SOUTH 3	187.5 to 202.5
SOUTHWEST 1	**202.5 to 217.5**
SOUTHWEST 2	**217.5 to 232.5**
SOUTHWEST 3	**232.5 to 247.5**
WEST 1	247.5 to 262.5
WEST 2	262.5 to 277.5
WEST 2	277.5 to 292.5
NORTHWEST 1	**292.5 to 307.5**
NORTHWEST 2	**307.5 to 322.5**
NORTHWEST 3	**322.5 to 337.5**
NORTH 1	337.5 to 352.5
NORTH 2	352.5 to 007.5
NORTH 3	007.5 to 022.5
NORTHEAST 1	**022.5 to 037.5**
NORTHEAST 2	**037.5 to 052.5**
NORTHEAST 3	**052.5 to 067.5**
EAST 1	067.5 to 082.5
EAST 2	082.5 to 097.5
EAST 3	097.5 to 112.5
SOUTHEAST 1	**112.5 to 127.5**
SOUTHEAST 2	**127.5 to 142.5**
SOUTHEAST 3	**142.5 to 157.5**

Those Living in Apartments

If you live in an apartment you should consider the direction of the main door into the apartment building and use this – the main door of the whole building – to identify the relevant natal chart of the building. Do not forget to check when the building was built or when it was last renovated.

Then, using the same natal chart you can superimpose it onto your apartment to undertake your analysis.

You should also identify where your apartment is located in the sense of which palace or sector grid in the building's *Lo Shu* chart your apartment is located. This will immediately give you the general idea of the luck of your apartment for the year, since you can see instantly if the numbers in that grid are auspicious or not.

In Flying Star feng shui there is also the concept of *"big tai chi"* and *"small tai chi."* Big *tai chi* refers to the whole *Lo Shu* square superimposed on the whole building, while small *tai chi* refers to the same *Lo Shu* square superimposed on individual apartments and rooms.

Thus to investigate the luck of your apartment, you should use the same natal chart (as defined by the orientation of the whole building) and superimpose it onto your apartment. You must identify the direction of your apartment so that you will be able to identify the different palaces inside your apartment for purposes of analyzing its feng shui.

This is also the method to use when identifying afflicted corners that need to be remedied, or palaces that have been visited by auspicious stars and therefore need to be activated.

The dotted lines show how you can superimpose the *Lo Shu* square onto an apartment, thereby identifying the rooms that are located in each place.

This bedroom would be in the NE palace based on the compass.

The Combination of Numbers in the Natal Chart

Before reading the luck of the different sectors of the home, it is useful to familiarize yourself with a natal chart. Below is the Flying Star natal chart of a building that faces the direction south 1. Do not attempt to figure out from this chart how it was created, nor how the numbers were placed where they are. This will only serve to confuse you. The creation of a natal chart is a complex process and is not covered here. All you need to know is what the numbers stand for, what they mean, and how they can be enhanced or remedied.

This number is the annual number and it indicates the luck for the year →

The big number is the period star, also known as the main star number

This little number is the mountain star, which indicates the luck of relationships

This little number on the right is the water star, which indicates money luck

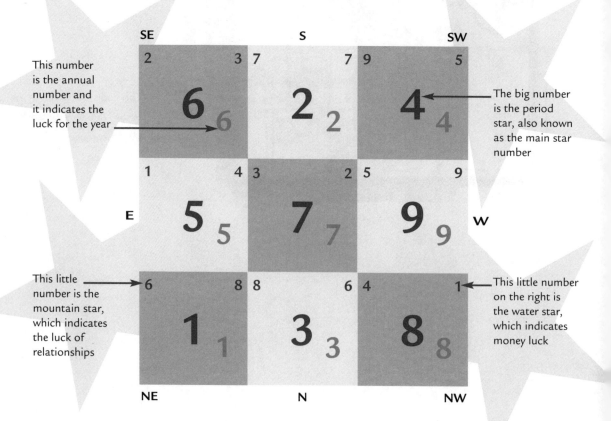

SE	**S**	**SW**
2 3	7 7	9 5
6 6	**2** 2	**4** 4
1 4	3 2	5 9
E **5** 5	**7** 7	**9** 9 **W**
6 8	8 6	4 1
1 1	**3** 3	**8** 8
NE	**N**	**NW**

☆ NOTE:

1. The combinations of all the numbers inside each grid are important. The little numbers on the left and right of the big central number are known as the mountain star (on the left) and the water star (on the right). These numbers indicate relationship and wealth luck respectively.

2. The interpretation takes account of how the annual numbers impact on the numbers of the mountain star and water star, as well as on the main period star.

3. Note that the water star is enhanced by the water element while the mountain star is enhanced by the earth element.

4. Note the elements of the numbers. Remember that these elements are based on the trigram placement of the Later Heaven arrangement of the *Pa Kua*. Thus 1 is water, 2 is earth, 3 is wood, 4 is wood, 5 is earth, 6 is metal, 7 is metal, 8 is earth, and 9 is fire. Take note of these number/element combinations and commit them to memory if you wish to become a feng shui practitioner.

5. Each of the directions has an element. Thus north is water, southwest is earth, southeast is wood, east is wood, the center is earth, northwest is metal, west is metal, northeast is earth, and south is fire. When a number flies into a corner always think "which element is flying into which element" and then ask yourself if the incoming element is enhancing, exhausting, or destroying the house element. This alone will offer you instant clues as to whether the number flying into any sector is good or bad.

6. The result or outcome of numbers coming into a sector can be auspicious or inauspicious. If they are inauspicious they can always be corrected! How? With the correct use of element analysis.

7. The combinations of mountain and water stars can be analyzed to indicate if they are auspicious or inauspicious. How good a feng shui practitioner you are depends upon your judgment of how bad a situation is, and, based on that analysis, what you can do about it. This is where the recommendations made can be very powerful.

8. Note the impact of the time stars. Each day, week, month, year, and each 20-year period has different flying star numbers ruling. These time stars exert their influence on the sectors and, when there is a concentration of bad stars on a particular day, week, or month, then any negative or positive effect is considerably empowered. Based on this, stars are never always good or always bad. It all depends on other stars combining with them.

9. Finally, when bad stars or good stars combine they sometimes need a catalyst – an external feature or structure - to trigger an effect. It's a little like karma ripening at a particular moment in time. Thus external forms and structures combine with flying stars to speed up good and bad effects. Similarly, symbolic decorative pieces can have the same triggering effect. So when a bad annual star flies into a sector with unlucky natal chart numbers, bad luck gets triggered much faster if the sector is also being hurt by a poison arrow.

Before proceeding to the detailed readings of the sectors of all the different houses, it is a good idea to briefly familiarize yourself with the meanings of the natal chart combination of numbers. The table given in the following two pages refers to the combinations of mountain and water star numbers. This table is generally similar to the one given in Part Two but there are instances where the combinations yield slightly different meanings.

Table of the Meanings of Combinations of Numbers

Mountain star	Water star	Indicated divinations and outcomes of the combination	Enhancers for good luck combinations or remedies for bad luck combinations
1	2	Marriage problems and danger of losses. Water in mountain is a sign of grave danger, just as mountain falling into water is a very bad sign indeed	Use plants to exhaust the water and strengthen the earth element
2	1	The matriarch is too strong, leading to marital problems	Use metal to exhaust
1	3	Wealth and fame luck are indicated	Use water to enhance and water plants
3	1	Prosperity luck is so good, if you don't have the karma/luck to live in this home you will change residence	Plant a bamboo grove to strengthen your luck
1	4	Political luck. Media and publicity luck. Romance luck	Use slow-moving water but not too much
4	1	Romance luck but too much water leads to sex scandals. Affairs leading to unhappiness and breakup of family.	Use a plant to strengthen wood
1	5	Health problems relating to the kidneys	Use a windchime
5	1	Hearing problems and also sex-related illness	Use a windchime
1	6	Auspicious. Intelligence with great commercial skills	Enhance with metal
6	1	Financial luck and high achievers in the family	Enhance with metal

Mountain star	Water star	Indicated divinations and outcomes of the combination	Enhancers for good luck combinations or remedies for bad luck combinations
1	7	Good money luck in period of 7 only, in period of 8 this combination means loss of wealth	Enhance with crystals or gem tree
7	1	Extremely good prosperity luck	Use a water feature
1	8	Excellent wealth luck into 8 period	Enhance with crystals
8	1	Excellent and auspicious luck. Money and family luck	Enhance with water
1	9	Good combination but can turn bad when 5 flies in	Do not enhance
9	1	Same as above	Same as above
2	3	Arguments and misunderstandings of the most severe kind. Backstabbing, hatred, legal disputes. Inauspicious	Use still water to cool tempers. Do not disturb
3	2	As bad as above and can get dangerous for those in politics. Tendency to obesity	Some masters recommend using gold and fire
2	4	Wives and mothers-in-law quarrel and fight. Disharmony	Use water
4	2	Illness of internal organs. Husband has affairs	Use water
2	5	Extremely inauspicious. Total loss and catastrophe. This is one of the most dangerous combinations in Flying Star technology, and when the 5 flies in, anyone staying here could suddenly have an accident or develop a terminal illness.	Use windchimes (plenty). Beware – do not have fire or could result in death
5	2	Misfortunes and extreme bad luck. Illness may be fatal	Use a windchime

Mountain star	Water star	Indicated divinations and outcomes of the combination	Enhancers for good luck combinations or remedies for bad luck combinations
2	6	Very easy life of ease and leisure. This auspicious combination is spoilt if a five-rod windchime is placed here.	Do not spoil the luck here with windchimes. Said to attract earth spirits!
6	2	Great affluence and everything successful	No need to enhance.
2	7	There is richness and money during the period of 7 but luck of children will not be good. Problems conceiving children. Period of 8 everything is bad!	Use metal (bells) in period of 7 and use water in period of 8
7	2	Money luck dissipates. Children luck is dimmed	Use windchimes
2	8	Richness and wealth but there is ill health, although this is minor and can be remedied	Use water to overcome bad health star
8	2	Better than above. There is money luck	Use mountain principle
2	9	Extremely bad luck. Nothing succeeds unless remedied	Use water plants
9	2	Better luck than above	Use water
3	4	Danger of mental instability. Tendency to stress	Use bright lights
4	3	Emotional stress due to relationship problems	Use red to overcome
3	5	Loss of wealth. Severe cash flow problems. If bedroom is here, financial loss is severe. If kitchen is here, sickness is inevitable. Better not to stay in this part of the house	Exhaust the 5 with metal but not with windchimes or bells. Use copper mountain painting

Mountain star	Water star	Indicated divinations and outcomes of the combination	Enhancers for good luck combinations or remedies for bad luck combinations
5	3	Money troubles. Disputes. Bad business luck	Use yin (still) water
3	6	Period of slow growth	Use yin (still) water
6	3	Unexpected windfall. Speculative luck	Enhance with gemstones
3	7	You could get robbed or burgled. Violence. Not so bad in period of 7 but sure to get robbed in period of 8	Use yin (still) water
7	3	Grave danger of injury to limbs. Be careful	Use yin (still) water
3	8	Not good for children under 12 years	Use bright lights to cure
8	3	Move children away from this sector	Use red and yellow
4	5	Prone to sexually transmitted diseases. Breast cancer	Use water/mountain
5	4	Just as bad as above	Use water/mountain
4	6	Bad luck for women who will bear heavy burden	Strengthen earth element
6	4	Unexpected windfall for women of the family	Enhance with a windchime
4	7	Bad luck in love. Will get cheated by opposite sex	Use yang (bubbling) water
7	4	Taken for a ride by someone of the opposite sex	Use yang (bubbling) water
4	8	Bad for very young children	Use lights to combat

Mountain star	Water star	Indicated divinations and outcomes of the combination	Enhancers for good luck combinations or remedies for bad luck combinations
8	4	Overpowering matriarch. Love lives of younger generation will suffer from the wiles of the mother	Use fire or red to overcome
4	9	A time for preparation. Good for students	Use wood or plants
9	4	Good luck for those starting new business	Use water to enhance
5/7	7/5	Problems caused by excessive gossiping. Danger of poisoning or anything to do with the mouth	Use metal in period of 7 and water in period of 8
5/8	8/5	Problems related to the limbs, joints, and bones of the body. It is necessary to be wary of rough sports	Use yin (still) water to pacify
5/9	9/5	Bad luck and tempers. Excessive mental disorder or stress – there is unhappiness and dissatisfaction	Use windchime Water/mountain theory
6/7	7/6	Negative chi – "Sword fighting killing breath"	Use yin (still) water
6/8	8/6	Wealth, popularity, prosperity. Great richness. Probably the best combination in Flying Star technique	Enhance with water and make sure you have an entrance or window in that sector
7/9	9/7	Extreme problems during period of 8. All troubles will be caused through excessive vulnerability to sexual advances. There is also danger of fire	Use water or earth (big boulders) to press down on the bad luck

The Use of Remedies to Overcome Annual Afflictions

Here are some very useful general guidelines on how you can overcome annual star afflictions.

1. To correct financial problems, focus your remedy on the water star (*siang sin* – facing star). If the water star is auspicious, enhance it with water. If the water star is bad or unlucky, exhaust it with wood.

2. To correct health and relationship matters, focus on the mountain star (*chor sin* – sitting star). When the mountain star is auspicious, enhance it with crystals; when it is unlucky or bad, exhaust it with water.

3. To improve your feng shui readings and investigations, never forget the annual flying star afflictions – the Grand Duke, the Three Killings, and the Five Yellow.

4. Always look at the structures, levels, and roads in the landscape – these usually trigger the bad numbers. When the landscape is bad, they act as catalysts for bad luck to manifest and manifest quickly.

5. If in doubt it is better to do nothing, since wrong analysis of elements can make matters worse. You can also email me at ltoo@wofs.com and if I am able to I will clarify matters for you.

A South 1 House or Building

Facing 157.5 to 172.5 degrees

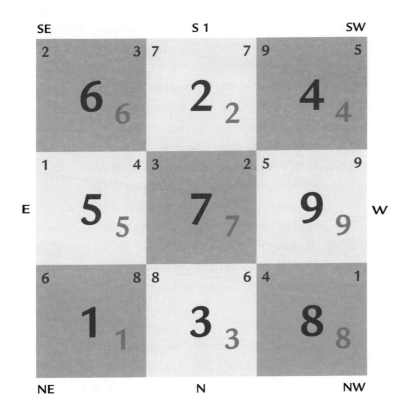

SE	**S 1**	**SW**
2 3	7 7	9 5
6 6	**2** 2	**4** 4
1 4	3 2	5 9
5 5	**7** 7	**9** 9
6 8	8 6	4 1
1 1	**3** 3	**8** 8
NE	**N**	**NW**

E (left)   W (right)

The natal chart for a **South 1** house in the year 2002 is shown on the left.

In the chart please note that the annual numbers in each grid are those in pink placed at the bottom right-hand corner.

The numbers in black represent the house natal chart. These numbers are also the period 7 numbers, and are referred to as the main numbers. The small numbers to the right of the main numbers are the water star numbers, while the small numbers on the left are the mountain star numbers.

General Outlook for the Year

Please note that the annual chart numbers are exactly the same as the period numbers in the year 2002. This is because the *Lo Shu* number for 2002 is 7, so the number 7 is in the center. The strengthening of the *Lo Shu* 7 does not necessarily bode well for a building where the main star 7 combines with the quarrelsome stars 2 and 3 in the center, as is the case for a south 1 house. Although 7 is usually considered a lucky number for this period, when combined with the quarrelsome 3 star it signifies the combination of metal and wood, which is a destructive relationship. With the strengthening of the 7, metal becomes ominous, so quarrels this year can lead to violence. It is a good idea to refrain from being too aggressive and hostile this year. The negative side of the year is the increased incidence of family quarrels. Women living in such houses tend to be bad-tempered throughout the year and need to learn to control their temper.

Illness afflictions are also indicated for the residents of this household, and this is due to the 2 star in the south palace. Despite the house enjoying the auspicious double 7 in the main entrance palace (south), illness luck causes problems. Hang a windchime in the south to try and overcome, or at least control, the 2 star in the entrance palace.

The women in this house will tend to have problems related to illicit romance. There could be too many opportunities for sexual misconduct, especially if there is water in the southwest palace of the house. This is mainly due to the 4 annual star meeting the 4 main star in the southwest palace, which can cause jealousy, insecurity, and mistrust between spouses.

Wealth Luck

Money luck is good and opportunities for promotion and improved income are excellent. The wealth luck of this house is steady rather than spectacular and there is no gambling or speculative luck, so please refrain from anything that has a speculative element in it. However, wealth arising from advancement at work is excellent, especially for the patriarch. The annual 8 star in the northwest palace helps him.

Health Luck

The double 5 star in the east palace suggests a susceptibility to flu and colds during the year for the children and those staying in this sector. The description in the texts is that of sickness stars affecting the growth of young children. This is compounded by the double 2 in the entrance palace, so that winds that enter the home bring illness and sickness. It is a good idea to be extra careful – do not bathe at nights and do make sure not to get caught in draughts.

Relationship Luck

The romance star enters the southwest this year, suggesting the possibility of love affairs, including illicit ones that will involve the women of the family. In households with marriageable daughters, this year brings marriage luck in that their love relationships stand a good chance of blossoming into marriage. But love also visits the more mature women of the household. Do make sure, however, that there is no water in the southwest since water will cause sex scandals.

The social life of residents also becomes very active and intimate relationships can be the result. This generally means that married couples living in this house will continue to enjoy a harmonious and happy relationship as long as there is no water feature in the southwest, while those who are single will meet someone of the opposite sex this year who will become significant in their life.

Those already in a relationship will see their love growing stronger and blossoming into a commitment. The palace with the most auspicious relationship star is the north, so if your bedroom is located here you will have stunning relationship luck this year. To enhance this, place an amethyst crystal geode under the bed.

Generally romance luck is excellent most of the year, although some slight hiccups should be expected during months one, three, and four i.e. February, April, and May. Romance luck reaches its peak during the second month i.e. between March 6 and April 5.

Prosperous Palaces

The most auspicious palace of the house continues to be the south palace, due to the favorable double 7, so it is an excellent idea to activate this sector with a water feature as well as a mountain feature. Place a small aquarium or a miniature fountain near the door on the left-hand side and also hang a landscape painting with mountains in it. Do note, however, that in 2002 the annual 2 strengthens the main star 2 to create a vulnerability and susceptibility to illness.

If you place a water feature in the south it should be very small and should be placed on the left-hand side of the main door (inside looking out). Please remember that water on the right-hand side of the door causes the man of the house to develop a roving eye, so it is a good idea to be careful about this. Roving eyes lead to infidelity, which in turn leads to marriage break-up. Guard against this – prevention is a lot easier than cure.

As for the mountain star, all that is needed to activate this is a small symbolic pile of stones in front of the house to symbolize the lucky mountain star. This will enhance the relationship luck of residents.

The northeast and northwest palaces of the home are also especially lucky this year. The northeast is already an extremely auspicious corner of the home with the 6/8 mountain/water combination, but the annual star 1 is also lucky as it strengthens the water star 8. Place a water feature here this year for increased wealth luck. Those who occupy the northeast palace could enjoy windfall profits that come from unexpected sources – either through investments or freelance work. Money and work come unexpectedly.

The northwest enjoys the annual star 8, which brings good fortune throughout the year for the house and for the head of the house. The 8 here signifies heaven bringing luck. It also indicates great good fortune for the family patriarch. Since 8 is earth and the northwest is metal, the number 8 is especially excellent. This is because metal is produced by earth. This will be true of all the houses this year. Northwest is a very lucky corner for everyone.

Dangerous Palaces

All houses are affected by the 5 yellow star, which in 2002 has flown to the east. Unfortunately the east also has the main star 5, and the combination of two 5s can, and usually does, have a deadly effect. This applies to all houses during the year, irrespective of their orientation. The effect of the Five Yellow is felt most in months two and eleven (i.e. in March and December), when the monthly 5 also visits the east palace. Anyone with a bedroom located in the east will be certain to succumb to illness. Keep plenty of fresh flowers in the east to strengthen its intrinsic element *chi* of wood, since this has the power to control the Five Yellow.

In a south 1 house, however, since the mountain/water stars of the east are auspicious, any bad energy brought by the Five Yellow will be considerably reduced. It is not advisable to place water here, however, since this could combine with the 4 water star to cause unfortunate romantic misadventures. But the 4/1 combination brings earnings growth to those in the advertising and communications businesses. This combination also favors writers and others engaged in the research and literary fields.

In the year 2002, the north palace is afflicted by the Three Killings, which bring gossip, slander, and minor accidents if activated. Thus you simply must not renovate your north palace this year. To do so is to invite accidents that could require you to be hospitalized. There could also be severe bad luck in financial matters.

Meanwhile, although the auspicious year star 6 has entered the southeast palace, this circumstance is unable to bring much good luck because of the fighting 3/2 natal stars there. Besides, the double impact of 6 (a metal number) in a wood palace does not bode well for this part of the home. Place metal windchimes to weaken the metal energy, and plants to strengthen the wood *chi*.

The south is afflicted by the Grand Duke Jupiter, which has flown to the south this year. Do not sit facing south and do not disturb the Grand Duke with digging, banging, or cutting down of trees in this sector of the home. This will cause the Duke to be disturbed thereby risking his anger, which manifests in severe bad luck. The Chinese refer to this as the "affliction of the year" and they are usually most respectful in observing the taboos related to appeasing the Grand Duke, whom they refer to as the God of the year.

The southwest and west both have difficult star numbers in their natal chart. The unlucky 5/9 combination needs to be controlled with metal windchimes, especially in the west which has the annual 9. This makes for an excess of 9, which is fire. Too much fire in the west destroys the metal energy here, causing bad luck to descend on anyone whose bedroom is placed here. The advice is to be careful of sleeping in these two palaces in the house.

Month-by-Month Analysis

☆ MONTH 1: February 4–March 6

The monthly 8 star enters the center palace, bringing happy events and prosperity to the home. Family gatherings are successful and happy. This is also a very good month for settling quarrels and misunderstandings. Do something positive in this direction and watch your problems subside. This is a year to be less aggressive, to be more conciliatory. The soft approach will win you friends and supporters.

The combination of the annual 4 and the month 5 in the southwest indicates many problems in relationships. This is not a good month for engagements or weddings. Those living in this house should wait for a better and more auspicious time before committing themselves to any relationship, as there could be unforeseen problems. It is also not a good month for giving birth and for anything to do with relationships. Married couples sleeping in the south will suffer from sleepless and problematic nights this month. They will argue for no apparent reason. Those sleeping in the northwest palace will enjoy advancement in their career.

Beware those occupying the southwest and northeast of this house. Sickness will befall those with Kua numbers 2, 5, and 1 (see page 253) residing here, although the illness is not serious. Those residing in the southeast sector will gain from the beneficial influence brought by the benevolent "father" in the guise of the 6 annual star. Those who are ill will also recover this month.

☆ MONTH 2: March 6–April 5

The second month brings good wealth luck, good investment opportunities, and career advancement due to the double 7 in the center grid of the natal chart. Investing in metal industries like cars, refineries, oil, and gas this month will bring some gains. Protect your career luck this month in the north by keeping an urn of *yin* (still) water placed against a wall.

There are three danger zones this month. In the south be careful of injuries and also heart problems. Use metal windchimes here to remedy and guard against the possibility of heart attacks. Those prone to them should move out of their rooms if located here in the south palace. Those in the west will have emotional problems. Stay cool and place a small urn of *yin* (still) water to calm the nerves. Also place six Chinese coins tied with black thread on the wall as a remedy. In the east there will be lots of sickness and the possibility of loss because of the double 5. Hang several windchimes to invoke the metal element as a cure. In this month all those residing in the east are very vulnerable. Move out of your room here if you can.

The northwest is especially lucky this month, with the occurrence of the triple 8. This situation rarely happens. If your room is here you can make investments with an easy mind since your luck is good.

☆ MONTH 3: April 5–May 6

This is an exciting month that indicates some small windfall coming to the residents of this house. However, there is also jealousy caused by women gossiping and quarrelling. Pay special attention to security because armed robbery is indicated in the northwest which will affect the family breadwinner – simply hanging a sword of coins in the northwest will solve this problem.

The star combinations in the south sector this month indicate the 1 month star flying into the 2 annual star – a sure indication of illness due to excessive money problems. It is a good idea to lie low and stay cool. Do not rock the boat. Do not take risks and, most of all, do not socialize excessively. There could be sickness but ailments are minor.

The southeast palace is extremely dangerous this month in terms of health. What is indicated is illness brought by the 5 month star and this is worsened by the 2/3 combination also in the southeast of this natal chart. The result could be headaches and severe migraines and even fractures of the skull. It's best to stay out of the southeast altogether this month. To reduce the danger, place a small urn of *yin* (still) water or place a ceramic *Kuan Kung* on a table.

☆ MONTH 4: May 6–June 5

This is a good month for the women of the house, but there is also danger of arrogance which can lead to losses being sustained. Those with the earth *Kua* numbers (see page 253) will benefit greatly if they live in the southwest corner of the home, but for all others this palace is fraught with illness and loss stars.

So basically the southwest is lucky for those belonging to the west-group Kua numbers. Fame and promotion are likely for them.

The southeast also has good career luck for those in the communication business. This is a great month for PR and advertising people if they live in this house. Those residing in the northeast will enjoy brilliant money luck. For them everything succeeds brilliantly and they will find themselves on a roll.

☆ MONTH 5: June 6–July 7

This is a very lucky month for this house because the 8 month star has travelled to the entrance palace. Health and career luck are smooth. The luckiest palace this month is the west, which benefits from the 6 month star. The southwest has wonderful romantic luck this month. Those in love should stay in the southwest and also activate it with love symbols such as the double happiness symbol and the mandarin ducks. If the main bedroom is located in the southwest be careful. There could be the entry of a third party into the relationship. The wife could look outside the marriage for love, and this might lead to a separation leading to divorce. In any case, there is some danger of adultery and infidelity. The recommended remedy to break the bad luck is to use a five-rod windchime to exhaust the intrinsic *chi* of the southwest palace.

☆ MONTH 6: July 8–August 7

This month is auspicious. Good luck comes from the 7 month star at the entrance palace. Open all the windows and doors in this part of the house. Those interested in gardening or who are engaged with planting will find this a most beneficial month for their plants.

The south palace enjoys excellent luck from the triple 7. The southeast is afflicted by the 2 month star and this combines with the palace's mountain/water star combination to cause severe bad luck brought about by noisy quarrels and misunderstandings. The west and southwest are also severely afflicted by the preponderance of 5/9s, which can be overcome only with powerful metal energy – use coins, bells, or windchimes.

Avoid staying in the west this month as there is danger of robbery and emotional shocks and trauma. Also avoid the southwest, since this location indicates arguments and lawsuits.

☆ MONTH 7: August 7–September 8

This is a month that favors both the men and women of the household. It is a good time for work and almost all the rooms indicate a lessening of bad luck and a flowering of good luck. The east, however, will have particularly bad problems. Cash flow difficulties, illness, loss, and cheating people will be inevitable. The remedies powerful enough to overcome these bad indications are the windchime and the curved knife. However, these will also "kill" the intrinsic *chi* of the sector, so moving out of the east room temporarily is a better solution.

☆ MONTH 8: September 8–October 8

This is a month when the residents will suffer from sickness and accidents. There will also be problems with in-laws, especially the mother-in-law. Those in business will find it tough to collect their debts, especially if they occupy the south sector. The bad luck of the month seems to have no respite. The patriarch will also succumb to illness. The silver lining this month is that the matriarch will come to the rescue of this month's poor financial luck.

Those in the south and northwest palace will get sick. Placing a *Wu Lou* (the potent symbol of well-being) in these palaces will get rid of the illness *chi*. Meanwhile, those occupying the southeast could lose money due to indiscretions. Overcome this with water. A tortoise will also be helpful. Those occupying the east will encounter severe relationship problems, and must be careful of small accidents.

☆ MONTH 9: October 8–November 6

This will generally be a good month: good for academic and scholarly pursuits, good for career, and good for investment. This is also a good month to get married or engaged. The good palace this month is the southeast, where the 8 star enters, bringing income luck to the household. The dangerous sectors are the north and the west.

If your room is in the southeast there is good fortune. If you reside in the north palace of your house there is danger of illness, accidents, and major loss due to quarrels. The bad stars cause the good natal stars to get afflicted.

The northwest is exceptionally lucky this month, having all the good numbers. Anyone staying in the room here is on a roll. However, if your toilet occupies this sector it signifies mega bad luck this month, so be careful!

☆ MONTH 10: November 7–December 6

An excellent month filled with joyous occasions. The luck of the house is the same as month one.

☆ MONTH 11: December 7–January 4, 2003

This is also a good month, with good investment luck. Career advancement is also indicated. Luck is the same as in month two.

☆ MONTH 12: January 5–February 3, 2003

Good opportunities but gossip is prevalent. Danger of infidelity. Luck is the same as in month three.

A South 2 or 3 House or Building

Facing 172.5 to 202.5 degrees

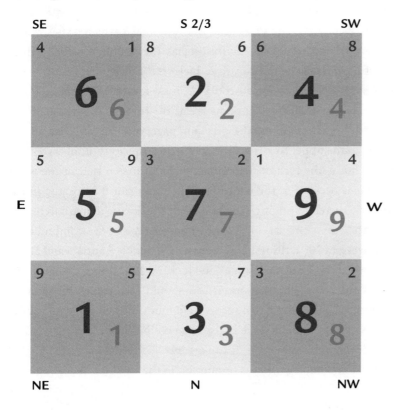

The natal chart for a **South 2 or 3** house in the year 2002 is shown on the left.

In the chart please note that the annual numbers in each grid are those in pink placed at the bottom right-hand corner.

The numbers in black represent the house natal chart. These are also the period 7 numbers, and are referred to as the main numbers. The small numbers to the right of the main numbers are the water star numbers, while the small numbers on the left are the mountain star numbers.

General Outlook for the Year

Please note that the annual chart numbers are exactly the same as the period numbers in the year 2002. This is because the *Lo Shu* number for 2002 is 7, so the number 7 is in the center. In a south 2/3 house the double 7 has flown to the back of the house and the entrance palace has the very auspicious 8/6 combination, which brings tremendous good luck. In 2002, however, the south palace is severely afflicted by the double 2 stars caused by the annual 2 and the *Lo Shu* 2. This brings illness luck to the house. However, if the door is located in the southwest or southeast palace, instead of the south, the indications for 2002 for this house spell great good fortune indeed. The southeast has the double 6, which brings wealth luck from heaven, while the southwest has the double 4, which brings wonderful romance and education luck. Hence there is money and relationship luck, as well as scholastic luck for the children. This is particularly true if all the bedrooms are at the front of the house. If you look at the natal chart on the previous page you can see that all the numbers in the upper first row (SE/S/SW) are auspicious numbers.

In this house the luck of the patriarch cannot match that of the wife's luck. This is because in the natal chart the water star 8 is located in the southwest, thereby bringing fantastic wealth luck to the matriarch. The northwest, in contrast, has the quarrelsome 3/2 combination. Nevertheless, in 2002, the northwest enjoys the double 8 annual and *Lo Shu* numbers and this brings awesome good luck. So 2002 brings good fortune to this house. This does not mean you should take things for granted. While money luck is good, there are certain months when you could suffer sudden setbacks. Equally there is also the possibility of receiving windfall profits during certain months. If you are involved in the management of a big project or company there is promotion in the air.

Wealth Luck

There are opportunities relating to promotion and advancement at work if your bedroom is located in any of the three sectors at the front of the house. The back room in the north also benefits from the double 7. Prosperity and income luck is said to be quite superb this year. Increases in real income could be significant. In fact, wealth luck is quite pronounced during the year, although how each household or building benefits depends very much on the exact location of the entrance door and the bedrooms. The southeast and southwest are luckier palaces than the south. The year favors men more than women in the income stakes, although women will benefit enormously if there is a favorable water feature in the southwest tapping the auspicious water star 8 there.

Health Luck

If the main door is placed in the south palace, the annual and *Lo Shu* stars 2 will bring illness *chi* to the household. This can be remedied by hanging windchimes here – the six-rod kind with hollow rods and made of all metal. If there is a *wu lou* (the potent symbol of well-being) incorporated into the design of the windchime it will be more effective. The other illness-afflicted palace is the east which suffers from the double 5. In fact, there are three 5s in this palace – the mountain star is also a 5. This suggests very severe health problems for anyone residing in this palace. It's better to move out of here this year since the gathering of 5s in this palace is like a time bomb waiting to explode. Illness in this case goes beyond headaches and migraines and indeed could even prove fatal. The other palace which could succumb to illness *chi* is the northeast, where the danger comes from an excess of water. Place some plants in this sector to control the excess of water energy.

Relationship Luck

The romance star 4 enters strongly through the southwest this year indicating a good time for love affairs to bloom into marriage. The social lives of the female residents become very active and intimate relationships can be expected to develop. Those who are married will enjoy harmonious and happy relationships, while those who are unmarried are likely to meet someone of the opposite sex this year who will become significant in their life. Those already in a relationship will see their love growing stronger and blossoming into a commitment.

Generally romance luck is excellent throughout the year, although some slight hiccups may be expected along the way. The mountain star 8 at the south sector brings a surfeit of good relationship luck, especially if it is also the entrance palace and the door is located here. Strengthen this further by placing a crystal (rose quartz) in this palace. The problem with the southwest, in contrast, is that with the water star 8 there it is excellent to place a water feature here, but doing so will lead to sexual escapades that can cause long-lasting problems for the marriage. So this will be a dilemma for residents of this house.

Prosperous Palaces

The southwest palace of this home is the sector with the best potential money luck. This is due to the placement of the water star 8 here. Having a water feature here can activate this but, as has already been pointed out, doing so this year could activate the 4 star in a way that leads to sex scandals. Even without activating the water star there should be relatively good fortune throughout the year. Those in politics or seeking power and authority should, if necessary, move to the room in the south sector since the numbers here favor fame and power in the year of the water horse. Strengthen this further with bright lights.

Anyone with rooms in the southeast, south, southwest, or north palaces will enjoy good income luck, and gain from investment profits or from a small business. Energize any of these sectors with music and activity and you should see money flowing in.

The southeast palace is visited by the auspicious 6 star this year. Money luck is therefore strong in the southeast. More wealth can be generated through investments and stock market-related pursuits. Activate the southeast with active *yang* (bubbling) water this year. Put all the auspicious symbols that signify wealth in this corner. Thus the golden sailing ship filled with cargo will enhance those in business, and placing a crystal ball will benefit those active in the stock market. Placing wealth gods here will also be most beneficial.

Dangerous Palaces

All houses are affected by the 5 yellow star, which in 2002 has flown to the east. Unfortunately the east has the main star 5 and the combination of two 5s can, and usually does, have a deadly effect. This applies to all houses during the year, irrespective of their orientation. The effect of the Five Yellow is felt most in months two and eleven (i.e. in March and December), when the monthly 5 also comes visiting the east palace. Anyone with a bedroom located in the east will be certain to succumb to illness. Keep plenty of fresh flowers in the east to strengthen its intrinsic wood element *chi*, since this can control the Five Yellow. It is vital that you hang at least six windchimes that have six rods each. The metal sounds and energy will exhaust the power of 5, thereby diluting its killing effect.

The other danger palace is the northeast, which has the 9/5 combination. This too can be controlled with the windchime. Meanwhile, the north palace is afflicted by the yearly Three Killings, which usually brings gossip, slander, and minor accidents. Do not activate the north this year. If you have water here, make it *yin* water i.e. water that is still and quiet. There should not be any renovations done to this part of the house this year.

The Grand Duke Jupiter is in the south this year, so this sector should also not be disturbed with cutting, digging, or renovation work. Keep the south quiet.

Month-by-Month Analysis

☆ MONTH 1: February 4–March 6

The monthly 8 star enters the center palace, bringing good wealth luck as it combines favorably with the year 7. However, the center is also occupied by the 3/2 stars which suggest things small. Since there is also the 3/2 combination in the northwest these quarrels will be between father and son over trivial matters. The month 9 star interacting with the 8 main star of the northwest in the house natal chart causes this situation of conflict. It is important not to strengthen either water, metal, or fire during this month. To do so is to run the risk of the conflict between father and son escalating into something more serious. This is not a good month for marriage. The entrance also has the 2/3 combination, this time made up of the annual and month stars. So this month is a quarrelsome month indeed.

Move your young children away from the southwest sector this month or they will get sick. And also be careful of the northeast palace, where illness could befall young children.

☆ MONTH 2: March 6–April 5

This is a lucky month. There is very good money luck brought by the double 7 combination of month and year stars in the center of the house. Good investment opportunities abound. There is also fruitful recognition at work for all residents. It is a good time to invest in land and property. Career luck is also strong, so go for it – ask for a raise and push for that promotion, especially if you are the man of the house. This is because the northwest palace is especially auspicious this month. The double 8 brings enormous good fortune. Those with *Kua* numbers of the west group (see page 253) will benefit enormously from sleeping in the northwest of the house this month.

The danger stars for the month reside in the south, where the double 2 brings illness, and in the east, where the double 5 brings losses and accidents. Stay clear of these two palaces.

☆ MONTH 3: April 5–May 6

This is an average month which brings some tension to the women of the household. There is jealousy brewing among peers. It is a good idea to pay special attention to security because there is the possibility of armed intrusion. Keep the south well lit at all times.

The west palace is lucky this month. It is good for work relating to gold. The north sector is afflicted by quarrelsome and illness stars - a 3/2 combination which brings some problems to the sector. Keep your back door closed.

☆ MONTH 4: May 6–June 6

In this month the men of the household will dominate events. There will be a great deal of activity and opportunity for the household to take a quantum leap in fortunes. The patriarch and the sons of the family will be demanding and arrogant, and in this month they will tend to be especially difficult because they will be under stress. However, it is stress of a good kind and will lead to good outcomes. Women should keep a low profile this month and indeed could fall ill. They are strongly advised to lay low and not socialize too much this month as it could lead to problems. This is definitely not a good month to get married.

The northeast will be extremely lucky, especially for those with west-group *Kua* numbers. Money and promotion are likely for them. Anyone residing in this palace of the house will enjoy good business and career luck.

☆ MONTH 5: June 6–July 7

A very lucky month for this house because the south palace, which is the entrance palace, has the month star 8 coming in to create a good combination with the annual star 2. Together they make the sum of ten, thereby bringing good *chi* to the mouth of the home. Business and career are favorably affected by the month star. Health-wise the month sees the 2 illness star flying into the afflicted east, so stay clear of the east. Keep this part of the home very quiet. Anyone residing here should have a medical checkup. The southwest has wonderful romantic luck this month, although there is also danger of sexual misconduct. Remember that too much of a good thing is usually dangerous, so do not let your heart get carried away.

If the main bedroom is located in the northwest, be careful of contracting an illness. This is because the 5 month star has flown in to the northwest. The northeast enjoys good fortune this month with a surfeit of 1s. This indicates plenty of money coming in to whoever resides in this sector. Make sure you have a windchime here to combat the unfavorable water/mountain star combination. This will enable the auspicious 1 stars to bring in the good fortune.

☆ MONTH 6: July 7–August 8

An averagely auspicious month. Good luck comes from the north direction. Open all the windows and doors in this part of the house. Those interested in gardening or who are engaged with planting should note that this is a most beneficial month for your plants.

The northwest palace is excellent for study luck. The northeast is excellent for career and business, and the east enjoys some income luck.

Avoid staying in the west this month as there is danger of sickness, robbery, and violence. Hang a windchime here to overcome the bad combination of numbers. Also avoid the southeast, since this location indicates illness this month.

☆ MONTH 7: August 8–September 8

This is a month of arguments caused by the men of the household. It is not a good time for starting a new business, since all the rooms indicate some problem or another. The southwest is the only room with good income and profits luck. Loss of money is due to bad decisions and poor judgment. Be careful of miscarriage and stomach problems, and be careful of accidents if you stay in the east palace.

☆ MONTH 8: September 8–October 8

This is a month when the household succumbs to illnesses and severe problems caused by the combination of 2/5 in the entrance palace of the south. The women of the household could suffer from robbery and violence. They will also be depressed. There are problems with the mother-in-law and from parents. The month brings little good luck to any sector, although the money situation is not a cause for concern for those staying in the northwest palace. The southeast part of the house has the potential of patronage luck ripening for the resident here.

Residents of the south palace will get sick. Placing a *Wu Lou* here will soften this affliction. Those occupying the southwest could lose money due to indiscretions. Overcome this with water. Keeping a tortoise (real or fake) here will be very helpful. Those occupying the northeast will encounter some misfortune. Overcome this affliction by placing the image of a dragon on a table in this palace.

☆ MONTH 9: October 8–November 7

This is a good month for those staying in the southeast and northwest palaces of the house. Both sectors have favorable star numbers that bring excellent prosperity luck. Those in the south will enjoy good luck in academic and scholarly pursuits. It is also a good month for career advancement and for making new investments. This is also a good month to get married.

The dangerous sectors this month are the east, whose residents could get robbed or hurt in a burglary attempt; the north, which has the unfortunate 5 star; and the west, where the illness star 2 is expanded by the annual 9 star. Illness thus afflicts those residing in the west.

If you reside in the east or west palace of your house there is enormous danger of illness, accidents, and major loss. Either move out completely for this month or, if you are unable to do so, use masses of metal to help reduce the problems. Definitely hang a six-rod windchime. Also, swipe the air in the east direction with a curved knife six times for six days in a row.

☆ MONTH 10: November 7–December 6

An excellent month, when wealth luck visits. The lucky and unlucky sectors are the same as month one.

☆ MONTH 11: December 7–January 4, 2003

Also a good month, with good investment luck. Career advancement is also indicated. The lucky and unlucky sectors are the same as month two.

☆ MONTH 12: January 5–February 3, 2003

Good opportunities. Danger of jealousy getting out of hand. The lucky and unlucky sectors are the same as month three.

A North 1 House or Building

Facing 337.5 to 352.5 degrees

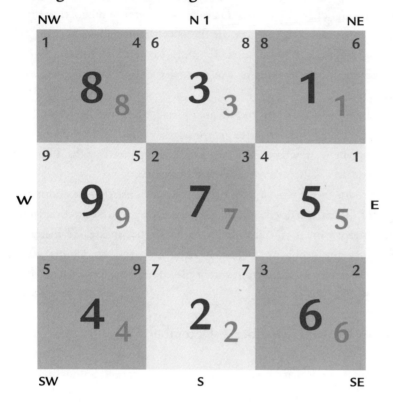

The natal chart for a **North 1** house in the year 2002 is shown on the left.

In the chart please note that the annual numbers in each grid are those in pink placed at the bottom right-hand corner.

The numbers in black represent the house natal chart. These numbers are also the period 7 numbers, and are referred to as the main numbers. The small numbers to the right of the main numbers are the water star numbers, while the small numbers on the left are the mountain star numbers.

General Outlook for the Year

Please note that the annual chart numbers are exactly the same as the period numbers in the year 2002. This is because the *Lo Shu* number for 2002 is 7, so the number 7 is in the center. The strengthening of the *Lo Shu* 7 is not necessarily a good thing for a north-facing house with the 2/3 combination in the center of the natal chart. The house will generally have moderate good fortune during the year with the occasional setback.

It is advisable to be very wary of the west this year since the water star 5, which brings accidents, loss, and failure, is strongly magnified by the three 9s in the chart. A combination of 5 and 9 is bad but with three 9s the effect is very strong indeed. The advice is to stay out of the west, especially during the sixth month when the monthly 5 visits the west. In this house the affliction of the Five Yellow in the east palace is modified by the 4/1 combination of mountain and water stars. So danger lurks only in months two and eleven.

North 1 houses enjoy good stars in the front palaces. All the rooms at the front of the house enjoy good fortune. The northwest has excellent relationship and career stars that are strongly supported by the annual and *Lo Shu* stars of 8. The center, which is the north palace, has the auspicious water star 8, while the northeast has the mountain star 8. So all these three sectors of the house enjoy good fortune. Wherever the door is located promises to bring good luck to the house. The prosperity luck for this house is strong although there will be occasional setbacks. Those involved in the real estate and construction business will do well. Also those engaged in tiles, crockery, and hardware businesses will have few problems.

Wealth Luck

The main advantage of this house is that its door direction benefits from the auspicious water star 8, which brings prosperity luck, wealth, and success in business and commercial ventures. This is further strengthened by an equally auspicious mountain star 6, which suggests that most ventures will move forward smoothly. The mountain star always brings good relationship luck when the number is auspicious. So this house benefits from excellent flying star *chi* at its main entrance door. Money will never be a problem in this house, especially if there is a pool or water feature in front of the house.

During the year 2002 the auspicious 8 stars are in the northwest sector, which benefits the family patriarch. This also suggests that there is a great deal of favorable heaven luck and the residents will benefit from the influence of powerful friends who will be most helpful. The northeast palace also has the favorable stars 1, 6, and 8, with the 1 being especially prominent. So once again money luck is not lacking.

Health Luck

The health luck of this house is average and there are no seriously bad sectors. The most troublesome is the east, which has the annual and *Lo Shu* 5 to contend with, but this should not be a serious problem.

More worrying is the 6 star in a *Kan* environment i.e. in the north. Appearing as a mountain star, it can sometimes be the cause of brain damage due to head injuries or illness but this happens only when *Kan*, the trigram of water, is contaminated by the 5 yellow star. This happens when the month 5 comes into the north, which occurs in the ninth month. So residents are urged to be extra careful during this month. There could even be blood injuries and problems related to the lungs and respiratory system. The advice is to hang a six-rod windchime in the north palace, since metal exhausts the earth element of the 5 star.

The two sectors with the 5/9 and 9/5 combination, i.e. the west and southwest, are afflicted with illness *chi*. These two palaces will benefit from metal windchimes and metal coins, since the earth element is afflicted. Residents sleeping in these two palaces must use this feng shui remedy.

Relationship Luck

For the single men and women of this house this is a good year to get married, and it is even better if you can select a particularly auspicious date. The best months for residents of this household seem to be the second or eleventh months i.e. March or December. Do not have too loud a wedding dinner, though.

If you stay in the west or southwest palaces look out for troublemakers who may wish to spoil your love relationship. Third party interference can sow discord. So those staying in the northeast benefit tremendously from the mountain star 8 located in this sector.

Prosperous Palaces

With a north-facing door and orientation, all the front rooms have very prosperous palaces. If you reside in the northwest, north, or northeast, you enjoy very favorable flying stars in your house natal chart. All the numbers are conducive to wealth creation. These sectors are not disturbed by any of the inauspicious annual stars. In addition, because of the double 7 in the south, residents also enjoy popularity and recognition. There is acceptance by friends and business associates and ability to inspire loyalty from friends and staff alike. There will be no problems with employees. Communication is smooth and expansion can take place without difficulty. Those in a career will move to greater heights with the invaluable assistance from mentors (what the Chinese call *kwai yan*). You can also make profits from stock investments and speculative ventures. There is also lottery luck.

The northwest palace has wonderful writing luck and residents staying here enjoy excellent income from careers in the communication business. Wealth-wise the 1 annual star gives lots of support and unseen guidance. This star has flown into the northeast, where the mountain/water is also an auspicious 8/6. If you want to enhance your business potential, you should place a beautiful colorless quartz geode here to signify a wealthy mountain star.

Dangerous Palaces

All houses are affected by the 5 yellow star, which in 2002 has flown to the east. Unfortunately the east also has the main star 5, and the combination of two 5s can, and usually does, have a deadly effect. This applies to all houses during the year, irrespective of their orientation. The effect of the Five Yellow is felt most in months two and eleven (i.e. in March and December), when the monthly 5 also comes visiting the east palace. Anyone with a bedroom located in the east is certain to succumb to illness. Keep plenty of fresh flowers in the east to strengthen its intrinsic element *chi* of wood, since this has the power to control the Five Yellow. In a north 1 house, however, the east is not badly afflicted since the stars 4/1 go a long way towards overcoming the Five Yellow. This is because water and wood are able to control earth.

The west has the greatest potential for ill health and loss of money. If you are rich and in business, avoid staying in or having your bedroom in the west palace of a north-facing house or building this year. If your office is in this part of the building you will lose money! Also keep the west undisturbed throughout the year. This is because the 9s cause havoc, with the Five Yellow expanding their power to bring loss and tragedy.

Harmony is the major concern in the southwest palace. The annual 4 is very destructive, since it is a wood element star coming into the earth sector. However, 4 also brings romantic luck. Nevertheless, with the 5 mountain star, all relationships must be suspect. So the mountain star 5 will create emotional problems that cause anguish. Pregnant women are strongly advised not to sleep in the southwest area of the house. If you do so there is danger of miscarriage and premature childbirth. Or worse, there is a danger that the unborn baby could be afflicted. So please move out of the southwest!

The north is also afflicted by the Three Killings (also called *sarm saat* in Chinese). If activated, this causes you to be affected by gossip, slander, and minor annoying accidents. So do not undertake any renovations here.

Month-by-Month Analysis

☆ MONTH 1: February 4–March 6

The monthly 4 star enters the north palace, bringing love and good literary luck to the household. This augurs well for those who are in love and dating, as well as those who are in the PR or advertising or communications industry. The northwest continues to be lucky. However, the illness star 2 enters the northeast palace, bringing problems to the limbs. You will suffer from aches and pains if you live in this palace.

The northwest is auspicious so use this month wisely. Accept promotions and any offers that you get this month and do not allow personal affairs to interfere with your career advancement. Indications are that someone of the opposite sex could cloud your career opportunities so stay clear of romantic entanglements this month. Your career could be jeopardized. This is your best month so take advantage of it. The southwest will encounter illnesses due to the month 5 and there is thus excessive pressure. Anxieties over pregnancies are indicated.

✫ MONTH 2: March 6–April 5

This is a quarrelsome month. There is danger of misunderstandings escalating into lawsuits and legal entanglements. It is necessary to appease the quarrelsome 3 star by having an urn of *yin* (still) water in that palace. At work, conflicts and bitter arguments are likely to cause you anguish. Wealth luck fluctuates and you are advised to watch your investments with diligence. Your financial problems are due to the month star 9 creating fluctuations in the northwest.

✫ MONTH 3: April 5–May 6

Another quarrelsome month. The problems of the previous month continue into this month, although the 5 yellow star is doing less harm this month as it has flown into the southeast, where wood energy keeps it under some control. Money luck stabilizes to some extent. Investment in property and equipment could bring gains. My advice is to be careful and not be hasty.

Those staying in the northwest will be lucky with money, while those in the east palace will get plenty of attention from friends of the opposite sex. But please don't get carried away by it. Keep eyes and mind clear for the one perfect partner who could also come along this month. If you reside in the east, you will experience a high-flying (probably adulterous) romance, which will make you very happy but will cause severe problems for your career. There is danger of excessive romantic entanglements. This is caused by the monthly 4 star over an annual 5 star in the 4/1 east palace.

The west is badly afflicted and will have to endure loss and lawsuits. There is very real danger of being so short of money you could lose your home. Whatever you do, please understand you cannot be of any help to anyone and do not guarantee any kind of loan for anyone. Hang plenty of windchimes in this part of the house.

☆ MONTH 4: May 6–June 6

Generally a troubled month when the month 5 flies into the center of the house. There are two ways to interpret this. Some masters contend that when a bad star flies to the center it gets locked up, others maintain that it spreads its negative effects throughout the whole house. Actually the effect depends on the layout of the house. If there is a small room in the center of the house the star gets locked up, and if the center of the house is open space then the impact of the center number is felt throughout the house.

Those residing in the northeast will receive wonderful opportunities in business and career but you should not speculate. Another lucky sector this month is the northwest, which benefits from the assistance of helpful people. Those residing in the west must be careful as they could get conned. And those residing in the southwest should watch out for health problems, particularly in the stomach and womb areas.

☆ MONTH 5: June 6–July 7

This is a tense month for the household. Complications and severe problems arise from quarrelsome business associates. There is danger of being cheated and betrayed by those you trust, especially if you are residing in the northwest. It's better not to trust anyone this month. The east is especially afflicted this month and great caution is urged if your bedroom is located here. Those residing in the southeast could find themselves embroiled in disputes over trivial matters. They should avoid getting hooked into other people's problems and power struggles. Those staying in the north will continue to suffer hostility from people.

The most auspicious palace this month is the south, where the 8 star has flown. Those residing here will enjoy good money luck.

☆ MONTH 6: July 7–August 8

This is a good month indeed for this house. The month star 8 flies into the entrance palace, bringing good fortune to the household. The head of the family will continue to have good fortune. The northwest palace is auspicious as the month 4 combines well with the annual 8. Once again, the west palace is afflicted with the 5 month combining with the annual 9 – a powerful negative effect is thus created. Best to get out of the west for this month. The illness 2 is in the southeast and this combines with the water star 2 to bring problems related to sickness. Children are especially vulnerable. Hang a metal windchime to control the 2s.

☆ MONTH 7: August 8–September 8

This is certainly not a good month. Disputes in business arising from the patriarch's work activities could escalate into litigation. It is important not to succumb to gossip or impetuousness. Stubbornness could also lead to problems. The man of the family should also be careful of being enticed into situations that could bring problems.

The east and the northeast sectors are very trying this month so try to stay strong mentally and emotionally. The best feng shui tip I can offer you is to place plenty of metal in these two sectors this month. Windchimes, bells, and singing bowls are all excellent for controlling the killing energies of the Five Yellow, especially when it is strengthened by the month 9 star in the east. Another method is to keep windows in the east closed.

☆ MONTH 8: September 8–October 8

Oh dear, this is such an unfavorable month for those staying in the south palace. The month 5 combines with the year 2 here to create health problems for the household's south palace. When the back of the house is afflicted in this way all residents suffer. Use windchimes to overcome these troublesome earth stars.

Wealth luck is described as being as weak as a wilting flower. The good luck of the northwest is negatively affected this month, so it is a good idea to lie low regarding financial matters. Keep the house quiet and free of excessive *yang* energy.

☆ MONTH 9: October 8–November 7

This is a dangerous month for the house because of the month 5 entering the main door palace. Usually this can be easily controlled with a windchime but this time the windchime cannot be used because of the annual star 3. Instead, I suggest quiet metal. Use a painting that is made entirely of metal. Remember also that the north is the place of the Three Killings and it is advisable that children sitting exams should move out of here. The northwest has a good literary star in the water star 4 and this brings good exam results. Romance luck is good also in the northwest.

☆ MONTH 10: November 7–December 6

Good love luck. The lucky and unlucky sectors are the same as month one.

☆ MONTH 11: December 7–January 4, 2003

A month characterized by disharmony and quarrels. The lucky and unlucky sectors are the same as month two.

☆ MONTH 12: January 5–February 3, 2003

A month of quarrels once again. The lucky and unlucky sectors are the same as month three.

A North 2 or 3 House or Building

Facing 352.5 to 22.5 degrees

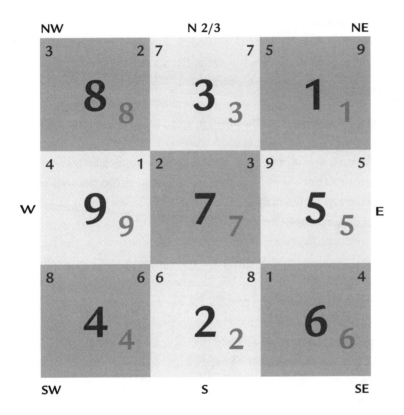

The natal chart for a **North 2 or 3** house in the year 2002 is shown on the left.

In the chart please note that the annual numbers in each grid are those in pink placed at the bottom right-hand corner.

The numbers in black represent the house natal chart. These numbers are also the period 7 numbers, and are referred to as the main numbers. The small numbers to the right of the main numbers are the water star numbers, while the small numbers on the left are the mountain star numbers.

General Outlook for the Year

Please note that the annual chart numbers are exactly the same as the period numbers in the year 2002. This is because the *Lo Shu* number for 2002 is 7, so the number 7 is in the center. The strengthening of the *Lo Shu* 7 is not necessarily a good thing for a north 2/3-facing house with the

2/3 combination in the center of the natal chart. This house will generally have moderate good fortune during the year.

This year, the extremely unlucky annual 5 star has flown into the east palace. This star usually brings calamities, accidents, and failures. You can also expect deceit, defamation, and instability in your position at work or in your company, especially if your bedroom is placed in the east palace. In fact, anyone staying in the east will suffer from a string of continuous bad luck all through the year. This is because the 5 and 9 combination is very strong in the east so you must hang lots of windchimes and create plenty of metal energy here. Note from the illustration on the previous page there are three 5s in the east grid. It cannot get worse than this! The annual 5 operates like a time bomb so it is important to take measures immediately to contain the dangerous alignment of 5s in the east. This also affects the sons of the family, as the east represents the sons. Growth will be severely curtailed. Do not let the danger in the east spoil the luck of the other sectors.

The three auspicious sectors of a north-facing house are at the back of the house, when the facing direction falls within the north 2 or 3 category of direction. This propels the double 7 to the front of the house, giving an auspicious configuration of numbers for the front door. The annual 3, strengthened by the *Lo Shu* 3, however, brings problems relating to quarrels. So although the double 7 is good from a money perspective, when combined with 3 it either means extremely good fortune (due to the sum of ten effect) or it can be spoiled if relationship problems get in the way. Then things could get contentious.

Wealth Luck

The annual 5 afflicts the east so severely that it could hurt the other sectors. Its negative impact could well spill over, especially if the east palace of the house is not separated from the other palaces with a wall. The severity of the 5 is due to the presence of so many 5s – as well as the presence of 9, which magnifies the bad effect. A good way to contain all this bad energy coming from the east is to use plenty of plants in that palace, and to paint the sector white. Windchimes and metal also work. It is not necessary to panic over this. A more helpful reaction is to be thankful for the warning and make certain you follow the advice given. The most important thing is to be careful and not take risks this year.

Elsewhere in the southwest and the southeast, however, the wealth luck is good. The southwest has a strong mountain star 8 and this is a most auspicious feature as it brings good networking luck, which brings better business prospects. Make full use of this by making certain an important room is located here. Then place crystals here to energize the auspicious mountain star. Those residing in the southeast will benefit financially from the 1 and 4 combination if they are in the communications and writing business.

Health Luck

In contaminating the east, the annual 5 also has a negative impact on the health luck of the growing children of the house. This is because it symbolically contaminates the growth energy of the home. The focus is on the 9 mountain star. According to the classic texts, the annual 5 coming in to the 9 mountain star in a *Chen* environment creates the danger of heart and kidney problems. The 9 is fire and this strengthens the deadly earth energy of 5. Children will be most susceptible; most in danger will be the younger girls of the family because *Tui* represents the young maiden.

The remedy is to create metal *chi* to exhaust the afflicted earth energy. If you find the *chi* to be too fierce you can also use plants, which have the ability to fight back more strongly against the Five Yellow.

In a smaller way the northeast is also afflicted; here the mountain star is 5, while the water star is 9. Once again the 5/9 combination is deadly so weaken it by hanging windchimes.

Relationship Luck

Love and romance for the young and single is not very promising this year. Pressure from work and problems at home could well place you in a dilemma and make you moody and emotionally unsteady. This will cause many unnecessary arguments with your loved ones.

Complications also arise easily for those who are married. The annual 5 is very unkind to relationships. Knowing this, you should try to be patient, thereby ensuring the marriage is not placed under too much strain. If there are disappointments, console yourself by understanding that all your bad luck will blow over by next year. Romance luck is strongest in the southeast sector where the 4 water star holds out much promise. The annual 4, which also brings romance luck, is in the southwest, so energizing the southwest will be especially fruitful this year.

Prosperous Palaces

With a north 2 or 3 orientation the palaces with the best money luck are the southwest, the south, and the southeast sectors. Residents should endeavour to reside in these sectors during the year, since the 5 star affliction in the east is particularly severe.

If you reside in the southwest you will enjoy romance luck. You will also be very lucky if you are a writer or in the communication business. Success, money rewards, and recognition are evident and will make you happy. Those working in advertising, PR, or research will enjoy higher status and success in their work. This is because the southwest of your house this year enjoys excellent communication luck. This is due to the visiting 4 annual star having flown into the palace this year. Stay away from water being placed here, however, since this causes scandals of a sexual nature.

The south and southeast palaces rate as second best, in terms of success luck. Residents of these two areas will enjoy good career and wealth luck, but the favorable outlook also comes with a warning to be careful. This is because the south is visited by the illness star 2. The southeast, however, benefits from the heavenly 6 star. So luck in the southeast is excellent this year.

Dangerous Palaces

All houses are affected by the 5 yellow star, which in 2002 has flown to the east. Unfortunately the east also has the main star 5 and the combination of two 5s can, and usually does, have a deadly effect. This applies to all houses during the year, irrespective of their orientation. The effect of the

Five Yellow is felt most in the months two and eleven (i.e. in March and December), when the monthly 5 also comes visiting the east palace. Anyone with a bedroom located in the east will be certain to succumb to illness. Keep plenty of fresh flowers in the east to strengthen its intrinsic element *chi* of wood, since this has the power to control the Five Yellow.

In this north 2/3 house the afflicted east palace is particularly badly hit because the water star is also a 5 and the mountain star is 9, which strengthens the 5. With the annual 5 coming in, the negative *chi* is so strong that everyone is strongly advised to move out of the east sector of the house. If there are bathrooms here, they serve to press down the bad luck. If there is a storeroom in the east, the effect is that the bad stars get "locked up." If there is a kitchen here, it also presses down the bad luck. However, if the stove is in this sector, the fire of the stove enhances it. Do please note that you must not dig, cut trees, or start renovations in the east either. If it isn't possible to move out of the east, hang six six-rod windchimes in this sector.

Meanwhile, please also note that the Three Killings is in the north, so do not renovate in the north. If you cannot avoid renovations, ensure you do not start or finish them in the north sector. Also, do not cut trees or make too much noise in this sector. Keep it quiet throughout the year.

Month-by-Month Analysis

☆ MONTH 1: February 4–March 6

The auspicious monthly 6 white star enters the east. This weakens the 5 star's bad energy, as a result of which bad luck is reduced. The other auspicious white stars are 1 and 8. The white star 1 goes to the west, bringing stable money luck to residents here, while the powerful 8 star flies to the center, bringing good luck to the whole house.

The lucky sector is the southeast, where residents will have the potential for upward mobility in their career and fairly easy success this month, due mainly to the 7 month star. Singles will be glad to hear that there are numerous opportunities to boost their love life, although this is not the best month to pursue romance. The 5 month star flies into the southwest, thereby afflicting the romantic star 4. So do not go overboard in your romancing or you might not like what happens next year. The south palace is afflicted by the 2/3 combination of annual and monthly stars so there will be quarrels and misunderstandings in this sector.

☆ MONTH 2: March 6–April 5

The monthly 3 star enters the north. When the month 3 meets the annual 3 in the north, where there is a double 7, a potentially explosive situation called the "volcano month" is created. Residents will engage in heated arguments. There is displeasure with one another. Be careful of fire hazards or robbery. These events are considered fiery in nature. Steer clear of romantic affairs and do not commit to anyone as it could affect your mental well-being and reputation. Love affairs will, in any case, be unpredictable because the 5 star brings instability this month in the east. You must stay cool. Do not make any hasty decisions. The auspicious location this month is in the southwest, where the double 4 makes for good relationship luck. There is also career success luck.

The residents in the northwest palace will enjoy job promotion and an increase in income. Some may receive windfall profits. This is because the northwest benefits hugely from the double 8 – both the annual and monthly stars are the auspicious 8. This benefits the man of the house. So in 2002 my advice to him is to go for it. Your luck is good and strong this year. It is not a bad time to consider making strategic investments.

☆ MONTH 3: April 5–May 6

Once again, this is a bad month. The illness 2 has flown into the north, where the entrance is. It combines with the annual 3 and the double 7 in a most explosive way. There could well be quarrels leading to injury and hospitalization. The indications of the flying stars are not good.

The east enjoys better luck this month than the past month, while the northwest enjoys good fortunes in the money area. The auspicious 7 enters the northwest and works closely with the number 8. The southwest has to cope with the 3 fighting star which means that relationships are in for a rough ride. It's better to stay above the fray.

☆ MONTH 4: May 6–June 6

This month the 1 star enters the north, bringing with it good luck which permeates the household. Meanwhile, the 7 star flies to the west and while it is generally a prosperous star for this period, unfortunately, when the 7 monthly star meets the annual 9 star, it turns evil and causes problems and illness related to the heart. This implies that there will be harmful negative pressure building up and hitting the residents.

Good luck enters the southeast, where the 4 brings good career and relationship luck. In the southwest, however, affliction comes in the form of the 2 illness star. If you have a door in either of these sectors of the home, the good and bad luck gets activated. You should use the door into the southeast and close the door into the southwest. The south enjoys wealth luck. Money and opportunities come easily. Finance is a breeze. The water star 8 is responsible for these positive aspects. In contrast, the year and month stars bring obstacles and problems.

☆ MONTH 5: June 6–July 7

Headaches, frustration, tension, anxiety ... this sums up the luck of the house this month. This is especially the case when the main door is also located in the north palace. On a happier note, however, income luck is improving. Be patient and wait for the right moment next month. Good luck is available in the southwest. Celebrations, reunions, and get-togethers are fruitful and advantageous. Investments will do well and people residing here will make good money this year.

The worst sector is in the northwest, where bad luck manifests itself in loss of money, bad tempers, and illness. Residents here feel angry all the time. It is the same for those in the east sector, where sickness and impatience will be the order of the day. There is simply no harmony. It is advisable to move out of here for a while to reduce friction in the household. Those in the southwest should be careful of falling in love too quickly. You might be setting yourself up for heartbreak. Go a little slower.

☆ MONTH 6: July 7–August 8

The luck cycle of the house improves significantly this month because the auspicious 8 star enters the north, reducing the pernicious influence of the 3 fighting star, as well as the Three Killings. However, if renovations are undertaken, bad luck returns with a vengeance. Another auspicious sector is the northwest. The monthly 4 and annual 8 here bring excellent success luck to careers and businesses.

In this month, the east palace is given a respite from the Five Yellow. With the entry of the number 1 star, the effect of the Five Yellow is considerably reduced.

☆ MONTH 7: August 8–September 8

Money luck can be as good as last month and may even improve. In the seventh month the auspicious 7 enters the north palace, bringing good luck to the household. The southwest is also extremely lucky, with the 8/4 monthly and annual stars. This means that those residing in the southwest will enjoy good fortune and ripening of wealth luck this month. This benefits the women of the household.

However, the dangers of the east sector return due to the monthly 9 entering the sector and instantly causing the Five Yellow to reignite! Stay away from the east. Meanwhile, the Five Yellow of the month has flown into the northeast, thereby bringing loss and sickness luck to this palace – if you are residing here lie low and wait for the bad star to fly out.

✲ MONTH 8: September 8–October 8

This month, the cycle of luck continues to be stable. At the entrance the white star 6 has come in, bringing some stability of luck. The south is badly afflicted with the 2 and 5 stars – these bring all sorts of unhappiness and illness. Hang a windchime to control these pernicious earth stars. If possible move out of this room temporarily, especially if you are ill. Staying in this sector will cause all latent illnesses to ripen.

The east is visited by the lucky 8, so this sector has a respite again this month. The northwest, meanwhile, which has had a good run for most of the year, now has to cope with the 2 illness star. There is therefore the danger of the patriarch falling ill this month, so it's a good idea to becareful.

✲ MONTH 9: October 8–November 7

This is a very dangerous month for the north 2/3 house. The danger is the result of the monthly 5 coming in to act as a catalyst that activates the evil side of the double 7. The annual 3 creates a situation of hostility in the backdrop. Watch out for robbery, crime, loss of money, injury (by metal objects), and disputes with the law/authority. People in status or power may lose their position. Please move cautiously and take special precautions. Do not travel too much because accidents can happen. Do not fight and do not argue with people. Be prepared to eat humble pie. Problems can be greatly reduced by closing all the doors in the north sector and not using them.

The east is also afflicted with the 5/7 combination, while the west suffers from the 9/2 combination. Both palaces are not lucky this month and it is a good idea to use remedies – a windchime for the west and a combination of red and metal for the east.

✲ MONTH 10: November 7–December 6

Mixed outcomes this month. The lucky and unlucky sectors are the same as month one.

☆ MONTH 11: December 7–January 4, 2003

A volcanic month. The lucky and unlucky sectors are the same as month two.

☆ MONTH 12: January 5–February 3, 2003

A bad month. The lucky and unlucky sectors are the same as month three.

An East 1 House or Building

Facing 67.5 to 82.5 degrees

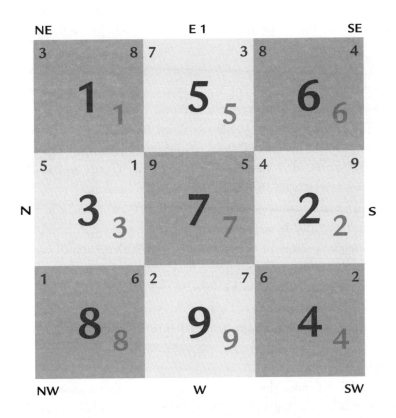

The natal chart for an **East 1** house in the year 2002 is shown on the left.

In the chart please note that the annual numbers in each grid are those in pink placed at the bottom right-hand corner.

The numbers in black represent the house natal chart. These numbers are also the period 7 numbers, and are referred to as the main numbers. The small numbers to the right of the main numbers are the water star numbers, while the small numbers on the left are the mountain star numbers.

General Outlook for the Year

Please note that the annual chart numbers are exactly the same as the period numbers in the year 2002. This is because the *Lo Shu* annual number for 2002 is 7, so the number 7 is also in the center grid. In an east 1-facing house the numbers in the center of the grid show a 5/9 combination which, when combined with the double 7, tends to have its negative influences activated and even strengthened. This is because although the 7 is the most auspicious star in this period of 7, nevertheless the annual 7 holds different attributes from the natal 20-year 7 star, and although it is lucky in the natal chart, some of its intrinsic evil influence will emerge when it is the annual or monthly star. (By the way, in the period of 8, the number 7 is deemed to be most unlucky.)

So for east 1 houses, luck is really not good this year because the annual 7 brings out the bad side of the 7 star. There will therefore be disappointments and life becomes a tiresome uphill battle. It is not a pleasant year. There are many challenges ahead. Be careful of burglary and robbery. Injury (getting hurt by metal or robbery) is quite likely, especially during the second and eleventh months. In the fourth and seventh months, residents should also watch out for health hazards.

There is, however, rather good romance luck this year, brought by the 4 annual star flying into the southwest. The northeast is also a favorable palace as this is the sector where the water star 8 is located. With the annual number 1 star flying into it, the water *chi* is strengthened, thereby bringing some good fortune to the sector. If you place a water feature in the northeast sector of the house, it will activate the good luck of this sector. The northwest is also a good palace, as the annual 8 star has flown into this sector.

Wealth Luck

The annual 5 star enters the east, so if your entrance door is here then the residents will be affected by the force of the 5 yellow annual star. The wealth cycle is seriously weakened this year because the natal water star 3 is also located here. In a simple analysis, we can already determine the quality of wealth luck. The deadly 5 star saps the energy of the water star, which has a wood element.

As the 5 also represent illness, loss, and injury, its coming into the east, where the 3 water star is, means that there will be a loss of wealth, and many quarrels and misunderstandings pertaining to money matters. So be careful of loss of wealth arising from quarrels and litigation.

There is, however, good wealth luck indicated in the northeast palace, so it is an excellent idea to relocate the entrance to this palace. If you are able to do this, your wealth luck will take a dramatic turn for the better. It is even more auspicious if you can build a water feature here – such as a small waterfall flowing towards the home. In terms of feng shui, this is the most effective action to take if enhanced income is your goal. Also place a fake mountain (a pile of stones or a large crystal) in the southeast corner of the home or of the living room, as this will greatly enhance the relationship luck of the residents, thereby ensuring that no law suits or court battles take place. This is because the mountain star 8 is in the southeast, which in turn is favorably supported by the annual 6 star.

Health Luck

The annual 5 is in the east palace where there is also the mountain star 7. The focus is on the 5 earth star coming in to a 7 mountain star. This strengthens the mountain star but since 5 is also a star that brings illness and bad news, the analysis here is that the 5 will cause the mountain star to turn negative, which is not good for health. There might be physical discomfort caused to the limbs. The problem is not serious but it will cause inconvenience. In addition, as the center grid has the 9/5 combination and the annual 7 is also in the center, the indications are that health luck is generally not good. Better to be careful.

Relationship Luck

The love scene for those of you who are single during this year looks promising. This is especially true for the young women of the house. They stand a good chance of finding someone suitable to love. So there is romance luck of the serious kind. Those who are married will also enjoy good ties with their spouse. There is harmony and happiness. The most promising palace for love is the southeast, where the mountain star 8 combines beautifully with the water star 4. Those residing in the southeast will find their social and love life blossoming in total perfection.

The appearance of the 6 annual star here brings good love and marriage luck from heaven. Since the southeast is also a sector that favors the young daughters of the family, the effect is that there are good indications of marriage possibilities in households with daughters of marriageable age. And since the east palace has an auspicious 7 mountain star, this indicates that potential sons-in-law will bring luck to the family.

Prosperous Palaces

The most prosperous sectors of this house during the year 2002, the year of the water horse, are the northwest and northeast palaces. The northwest sector has a fantastic configuration of white stars (1, 6, and 8) and these are the most auspicious stars of all. The very lucky water star in particular, if energized by a water feature, will attract plenty of money luck and this is enhanced this year by the annual 8 star. Since the luck of 6 means it comes from heaven, the good fortune experienced by those in this sector will be very real and long lasting. Residents of this palace will experience excellent income luck, recognition, and fame during the year. There are honors from higher-ranking officials and help from influential people. Mentor luck just flows. Those in politics and in business will be successful. Anything to do with gold and metal will succeed. There is an abundance of wealth luck. Health is also vibrant.

Meanwhile, the northeast also has an excellent configuration of stars, mainly the 8 water star which is in turn strongly supported by the 1 annual star. This highlights the strong influence of water, which brings prosperity and money luck. Those residing in this palace of the house will benefit strongly from the auspicious water star. It is an excellent idea to build a water feature that will activate the water star here.

Dangerous Palaces

All houses are affected by the deadly 5 yellow star, which in 2002 has flown to the east. Unfortunately the east also has the main star 5, and the combination of two 5s can, and usually does, have a deadly effect. This applies to all houses during the year, irrespective of their orientation. The effect of the Five Yellow is felt most in the months two and eleven (i.e. in March and December), when the monthly 5 also comes visiting the east palace. Anyone with a bedroom located in the east is almost certain to succumb to some kind of illness.

In a house where the entrance faces east or is located in the east palace, the effect of this negativity is multiplied. So do take care and keep plenty of fresh flowers in the east to strengthen its intrinsic element *chi* of wood, since this has the power to control the Five Yellow. Another good way to overcome the effect of the Five Yellow is to place six coins above the doorway or under the doormat, or hang six-rod windchimes near the side of the door. The use of metal weakens the Five Yellow, while the use of wood energy kills it. In feng shui we always prefer to exhaust and weaken rather than "kill," since this conforms to the principles of *yin* and *yang*. The west is the place to watch out for your health. Pregnant women or couples who wish to conceive a child may want to move out of the west room and use the southwest or southeast rooms instead. The west room is particularly bad for human harmony. There will be bust-ups and broken relationships. If this building is a factory, your workers will cause havoc and refuse to listen to authority. All this bad news is due to the combination of 2s and 9s here, as well as a 7 water star. This combination of numbers indicates danger.

Month-by-Month Analysis

☆ MONTH 1: February 4–March 6

The auspicious monthly 8 star enters the center grid and brings with it some good news for the whole household. This overcomes the ill effect of the natal chart star combination here.

The lucky sectors are in the southeast and northwest of the house. In these sectors, residents enjoy advancements in their careers. There is easy success this month. It will not be difficult to be successful in job applications. Interviews will go well and those playing the stock markets will enjoy reasonably good luck. For those who are single and staying in the southeast, there are opportunities for romance. The northwest enjoys good luck and everything is smooth. People pay attention to you and you are highly respected. The south palace is afflicted with the combination of 2/3 annual and monthly stars, bringing with it a great deal of aggravation and heartaches. Residents in this sector should stay calm and practice some meditation, otherwise they will quarrel with everyone.

The southwest is also visited by the 5 star which brings bad luck and loss. Romance for residents of this palace could turn stressful. Once again stay cool. It will get better in the coming months.

☆ MONTH 2: March 6–April 5

The auspicious locations this month are the northwest and northeast. In the northwest money and career luck are excellent. There is also the possibility of an increase in income, and promotion. Some may even be lucky enough to gain windfall profits. In the northeast there is a great deal of money luck brought by the 1 star. Romance luck soars this month and the southwest palace really comes into its own. Marriage opportunities will abound for the young women and men of the household.

The monthly 2 enters the south making it a double whammy. This has serious effects on the health of residents. Arguments and displeasure rule the day and these culminate in fever or heart-related types of illness. Resist being too high profile as developments may hurt your reputation. The 2 also causes setbacks in relationships. You should lie low.

The monthly 5 enters the east, also making this a seriously afflicted sector. The young sons of the family could succumb to illness this month, and overall the household could suffer from business setbacks and loss. Illness is also hovering at the edge of probability.

☆ MONTH 3: April 5–May 6

The romance luck of the house continues to be strong this month as the auspicious romance star 4 enters the entrance palace of the house and although the contentious 3 has flown into the southwest, nevertheless the numbers of the natal chart there are strong enough to prevail. The auspicious 1 white star enters the south, where it alleviates the illness star 2, making things a bit better in this palace of the house. The auspicious 8 star enters the west but here it cannot do much good since the other natal chart stars here are most unlucky. All endeavors move smoothly this month but there is little wealth luck.

The northwest palace continues to be healthy and vibrant. In the southwest there is a need for some restraint in emotional affairs. It is a month of the peach blossom when love blooms. Enjoy it by all means but do not go overboard as the monthly 3 star can cause misunderstandings to arise. In the east the 4 star brings some career luck for those in advertising, publicity, and media-related businesses.

☆ MONTH 4: May 6–June 6

The volatile 9 star enters the south palace, bringing increased bad luck for the health and vitality of residents there. In the southeast, passion for love affairs will heighten and this is fine since getting involved in entanglements is not necessarily a bad thing. There is heaven luck smiling on the romantic entanglements of residents here.

Good luck enters the northeast, the northwest, and the southeast. If you have doors in these sectors, use them. The northwest enjoys good power luck this month. Those in positions of authority and status will get their way. People succumb to your demands. The northeast has money advancement luck and those in business will benefit. Those in military or physical occupations (sportspeople) will also enjoy a month of success. Those in high positions achieve recognition. There is more money! Enhance it with a water feature to take advantage of the water star 8, which is being strengthened this month by the monthly star 8 also having flown into the northeast.

The southeast has the auspicious sum of ten combination formed by the annual 6 and the monthly 4. This brings wonderful romantic luck which benefits residents of this sector, as well as the marriageable young women of the household.

☆ MONTH 5: June 6–July 7

Luck takes a decided turn for the worst. The horrible combination of 5/2 this month brings bad luck to the entrance palace (east), which spreads throughout the household. It is vital to place some metal windchimes in the east to try and control the bad combination. This is the worst sector of the house this month. Residents feel uneasy and sickly, lack vitality, and succumb to bugs and common colds. Illness is to be expected this month. There may be accidents to those living in this palace so do be careful.

Other afflicted sectors this month are the northwest and the southeast, although the negative effect is not significant. Nevertheless, the patriarch should make sure he does not drive carelessly. The southeast sector is afflicted with the so-called "Bull-Fight Sha," which comes in the form of the 3 star. Those staying in this sector should (as the connotations of bull-fighting suggest!) stay out of conflicts and be firm about not wanting to get involved in other people's affairs.

☆ MONTH 6: July 7–August 8

This is generally a better month as the month star 1 has entered the east, thereby improving the situation in this afflicted sector. In the south the normally auspicious 7 brings bad luck as it combines with the 2 annual star. Luck here is not good.

In the north the auspicious 8 star has come visiting and this strengthens the auspicious 1 water star of this sector. The lucky palaces this month are the northeast and northwest, where the number combinations are auspicious. In the northeast, the 6 combines well with the 1 star – both are white stars, which bring good fortune. In the northwest, the 4 star indicates that there is excellent money luck, which favors those in the communication business. It can also mean that those residing in this sector could find love, romance, and marriage opportunities. The 4 is also a romance star number. The taboo is not to have water near the 4, as this tends to cause the development of scandals.

☆ MONTH 7: August 8–September 8

The outlook for this month is loss and discord, as well as problems associated with illness, accidents, and all other forms of bad luck. This is because the monthly 9 star has entered the east sector to activate serious problems arising from the double 5 combination. Since the east is the direction of the house, the negative impact affects all the residents. If the entrance door is in the east as well, the bad luck is really quite serious. The remedy lies in all-metal windchimes, as well as lots of coins and even metallic art hung on the walls. A side effect of the problem of the number combination is that the young will challenge the older generation and those in authority will face confrontation from subordinates. Household matters are in some disarray, while communication between parents and children is at a low ebb. Quite a bad month.

However, there is also good news. Romance for residents – especially for the women of the house – is most enjoyable. They will easily be swept off their feet by well-heeled admirers who will shower them with gifts. Marriage proposals are also likely because the intentions of those who woo the women of the household are honorable.

☆ MONTH 8: September 8–October 8

A much better month in terms of income luck, although most of the sectors do not have good combinations. The entrance in the east sector enjoys the auspicious 8 month star and the northeast has the good combination of 1/4, which brings good career luck for residents of this sector. The southwest also has a good combination of 4 and 7 stars but all other sectors experience either low *chi* levels or afflictions. The south is the most severely affected since the month 5 star combines with the annual 2 star, bringing illness, loss, and nothing good. This palace will benefit from a windchime – hang it here this month if you want to overcome the impact of really bad time dimension feng shui. Residents staying here will fall ill. Nursing mothers should not stay here, nor should young children who tend to be sickly. The severity of the 2/5 combination in the south is usually very terrible, because the fire of the south produces earth. Both the 2 and 5 stars are earth stars and strengthening them is akin to expanding their negative effect.

☆ MONTH 9: October 8–November 7

This month the violent 7 star enters the east palace and combines with the annual 5 to bring huge bad luck to the household. Although the 7 star is usually regarded as a lucky star in the present period of 7, nevertheless, as a time dimension star for either the year or the month, it is regarded as an evil star – especially when it combines with the 5 or the 2. In this case the 7 combines with the 5 star to bring the threat of robbery with violence into the picture. If you have a house with an east 1-facing door, I strongly urge you to beef up your security, as the danger of break-ins and armed robbery is very real. Take extra precautions. Keep a dog as this will be a strong deterrent. Also hang windchimes in the east and place an inverted broom outside your main front door.

The threat of armed robbery is also indicated by the 7/9 combination of annual and monthly star numbers for the center of the house. It is a good idea to place an urn of *yin* (still) water in the center of the house, as this will reduce the effect of the 9 monthly star there. The west sector is also afflicted by the illness star 2.

The lucky palaces this month are the southeast, where the monthly star 8 brings good money luck; the northwest, which enjoys the monthly 1 star; and the southwest palace, which has the auspicious 6 star. All three sectors indicate good vibrations for their residents so, on balance, as long as the proper precautions and remedies are taken to overcome the bad stars in the entrance, the luck of the household is not bad.

☆ MONTH 10: November 7–December 6

The lucky and unlucky sectors are the same as month one.

☆ MONTH 11: December 7–January 4, 2003

The lucky and unlucky sectors are the same as month two.

☆ MONTH 12: January 5–February 3, 2003

The lucky and unlucky sectors are the same as month three.

2002

An East 2 or 3 House or Building

Facing 82.5 to 112.5 degrees

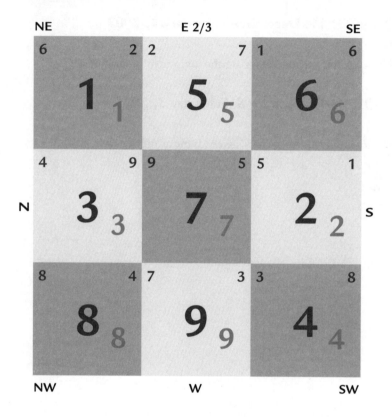

NE   E 2/3   SE

6 2	2 7	1 6
1 ₁	**5** ₅	**6** ₆
4 9	9 5	5 1
3 ₃	**7** ₇	**2** ₂
8 4	7 3	3 8
8 ₈	**9** ₉	**4** ₄

N   S

NW   W   SW

The natal chart for an **East 2 or 3** house in the year 2002 is shown on the left.

In the chart please note that the annual numbers in each grid are those in pink placed at the bottom right-hand corner.

The numbers in black represent the house natal chart. These numbers are also the period 7 numbers, and are referred to as the main numbers. The small numbers to the right of the main numbers are the water star numbers, while the small numbers on the left are the mountain star numbers.

General Outlook for the Year

Please note that the annual chart numbers are exactly the same as the period numbers in the year 2002. This is because the *Lo Shu* annual number for 2002 is 7, so the number 7 is also in the center grid. In an east 2- or 3-facing house the numbers in the center of the grid show a 9/5 combination which, when combined with the double 7, tends to have its negative influences activated and even strengthened.

At the same time, the annual 7 star flies into the center palace, creating a double 7 situation in the center. The 7 is the most auspicious star in the 7 period, but when it appears as an annual star it holds different meanings from when it comes as a natal 20-year period star. So although 7 is lucky in this period, its unlucky aspects will manifest themselves when it makes its appearance as an annual or monthly star. For the east 2/3 house, the center grid has the inauspicious and troublesome 9/5 combination which also brings out the evil nature of the 7. In addition, there are double 5s in the main door area, with a 2/7 mountain/water star combination – all of which suggest rather severe bad luck for this household during the year 2002.

The remedy is to place a six-rod windchime at the east palace both inside and outside the house. A metal six-rod windchime should also be placed in the center. These remedies are to control the negative 2 and 5 star numbers, which are the cause for the unlucky outlook for the house. It is also the 5 which brings out the bad side of the 7 star number. Also note that because it is the *Chen* (name of the trigram here in the east) palace which is the *ling san* direction of the 7th period, the 7 star will also emit negative aspects. So as a result, both the natal mountain star and palace itself do not have auspicious stars. You may also have to watch out for minor problems to do with fire, burglary, and robbery.

Wealth Luck

If your main entrance is located in the east sector, residents will be very strongly affected by the force of the double 5 star, which is featured both as an annual star as well as a *Lo Shu* star of the natal chart. This 5 star is most inauspicious when placed at the entrance to a household and it brings ill health as well as unpleasant happenings. In the case of an east 2/3 house, the natal chart also indicates a rather unlucky situation for the east palace. If this is also the entrance palace, luck for the whole household will generally be bad this year. The best remedy is to place metallic things in the sector – windchimes, metal coins, and bells.

The water star 8 in the southwest palace brings good money luck for the women of the household. Here earth is found in an earth sector so the

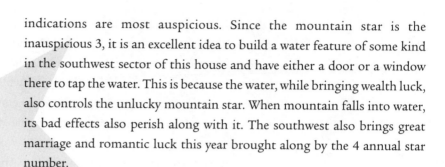

indications are most auspicious. Since the mountain star is the inauspicious 3, it is an excellent idea to build a water feature of some kind in the southwest sector of this house and have either a door or a window there to tap the water. This is because the water, while bringing wealth luck, also controls the unlucky mountain star. When mountain falls into water, its bad effects also perish along with it. The southwest also brings great marriage and romantic luck this year brought along by the 4 annual star number.

In the northwest, friends will help and provide support. The favorable mountain star here should be energized with the presence of crystals. Amethysts will strengthen love and marriage potential while stone boulders tied with red ribbons bring additional luck.

The southeast, meanwhile, has a combination of 1s and 6s, both white numbers and both auspicious. The unfortunate thing, however, is that 6 is metal while the southeast is wood. Since metal destroys wood, the luck brought in by the 6 does not do much to help the sector. However, as the 1 is water, it produces wood, so here the good and bad cancel each other out in terms of element analysis.

Health Luck

With the annual 5 coming into the entrance palace, where there is a 2 mountain star and a *Chen* environment, a most harmful combination is created. As a result of this configuration, health problems will emerge and physical fitness will take a major downturn. There could be ailments related to the liver and ears (wood element), which will lead to tension, anger, and temper tantrums. People in the household will benefit hugely from drinking water to help the wood energy in the body, which is being put under strain. There could also be sickness to do with the stomach or womb.

The best way to escape being hit by these health problems is to sleep in an auspicious room (for example in the southeast or the northwest), or at least move out of the east palace for the duration of the year. This will ensure that you will escape the health negativities. Alternatively, hang windchimes in the entrance palace as recommended earlier.

Relationship Luck

Love luck for the women and girls in the family appears to be most promising. This is because the southwest has so many good and auspicious star numbers. This year, the romantic star 4 is in the southwest. Also the water star is the auspicious 8, so the southwest looks very auspicious indeed. There could be a marriage in the household and this will be an occasion for rejoicing.

The northwest also has great romance luck and here it favors the men of the household. The water star here is the romantic 4 and the mountain star is the auspicious 8, so here the romance luck is brought by the natal chart star numbers. The northwest also has good romance luck and here it favors the men of the household. The water star here is the romantic 4 and the mountain star is the auspicious 8, so in this sector the romance luck is brought by the natal chart star numbers. The annual star 8 strengthens the good networking fortune brought by the mountain star.

Prosperous Palaces

The prosperous palaces in the house this year are the northwest, southeast, southwest, and northeast. Sleeping in any one of these rooms brings good fortune. All three palaces also have auspicious annual star numbers.

Those residing in the northwest will have success brought by the annual star 8. The northwest enjoys good wealth luck due to this, as well as the presence of the triple 8 combination of mountain, annual and period stars that brings an enhancement of success luck. Most auspicious.

Those in the southeast enjoy the luck of having helpful people coming into their life this year, people who will make important contacts and bring significant opportunities. There is honor from higher-ranking officials and help from mentors. There are tremendous opportunities in business and lots of good luck.

The southwest will receive benevolent relationship luck this year, brought by the excellent 4 star. Things go smoothly if there is a water feature here, but if there is not then there could be some problems arising from gossip and jealousy. Placing a water feature here is a good idea.

The northeast residents will benefit from the double 1 stars although the 2 water star could bring some health problems. Nevertheless, from a prosperity viewpoint, the northeast looks good this year.

Dangerous Palaces

All houses are affected by the 5 yellow star, which in 2002 has flown to the east. Unfortunately the east also has the main star 5, and the combination of two 5s can, and usually does, have a deadly effect. While the 5 brings bad luck to all houses, its effect in an east-facing house is a lot more serious simply because the period 5 is also located in the east. Thus there is a double whammy! For this house the Five Yellow is felt most in the months two and eleven (i.e. in March and December), when the monthly 5 also comes visiting the east palace. Anyone with their bedroom located in the east is certain to succumb to illness. If you cannot move out of the room, hang plenty of metallic windchimes with six hollow rods to control the Five Yellow.

In addition to the east, other danger sectors are the south and the center. The south sector suffers from the double 2 stars, as well as the 5 mountain star. This brings the danger of illness and problems related to the stomach, womb, and kidneys. Bad health luck in the south can also cause problems associated with energy being too *yang*, for instance problems with the eyes and the heart. It is a good idea to be extra careful this year.

Month-by-Month Analysis

☆ MONTH 1: February 4–March 6

In the first month of the year the entrance palace is visited by the white star 6, which does not bode well for the east sector – a wood sector. Wealth luck gets cut by metal. Meanwhile, the unlucky month 3 star enters the south, bringing arguments and tension between family members, and is especially harmful for anyone staying in that sector. At work there are misunderstandings with colleagues. The 3 star also affects career luck, so watch out for backstabbing in the workplace. The southeast enjoys benevolent good fortune.

The northwest enjoys good luck. People in positions of power will have their power and authority enhanced. Those climbing the corporate ladder will find moving up very easy this month. Superiors will notice them and give them a helping hand. Those in the north will enjoy the attention of members of the opposite sex. It is a time for romance. Those in the southwest should pay attention to their health. Remove young children from this room, or they will fall ill.

☆ MONTH 2: March 6–April 5

In the second month, the month 5 star flies into the east combining with the annual 5 star and also with the water star 7. This creates a very dangerously unlucky situation in the east. The natal chart also has the 2 and 7 stars so residents can expect fire hazards, emotional high tension, arguments, burglary, or difficult situations involving the keyword fire. Avoid getting romantically involved because it will affect your reputation. The 2 causes setbacks in all types of relationships. Those involved in the stock market should beware. This will be a rocky month of volatility. But the real danger is the threat of armed violence befalling some member of the family – very likely a female member. So it is a good idea to be very careful.

The southwest is auspicious. Opportunities for love and romance abound and income enhancements are just round the corner. Singles wishing to marry and currently living in the southwest will get the chance to do so this month. Those in the southeast will gain from their investments. Girls under 12 years, however, might get hurt.

The south suffers from rather severe health problems. Health hazards pose a serious threat this year. The northwest residents suffer a very minor setback this month. Those residing in the west will suffer severe financial problems brought on by litigation against them.

☆ MONTH 3: April 5–May 6

In the third month, luck improves. The lucky 4 star enters the east, bringing good relationship *chi* to the prominent 7 water star. All endeavors related to interactions with people will move smoothly this month. There could, however, be some danger of residents being conned by the opposite sex as this is the meaning of a 4/7 combination. This is a good month for negotiations and romance. Good luck enters through the front door. Prosperity luck is in the west this month and residents in the northwest continue to enjoy the good luck of the natal chart placement of stars.

☆ MONTH 4: May 6–June 6

In the fourth month, the 3 month star enters the east making it an unstable, quarrelsome month. Pay attention to the way you react and respond to people. Do not allow your tongue or temper get the better of your judgment, for in this month small words can flare into big trouble. Remember that major obstacles can arise from trivial matters that take a wrong turn. The 3 star always hinders progress. Money luck is also unfavorable, and also be careful regarding matters of the heart. Love relationships get very rocky this month. The 2 star entering the southwest is the reason for poor romance luck this month.

Good luck continues to bless the northwest as well as the northeast. If you have any doors in either of these sectors you should use them, as this activates good luck and is an excellent alternative to using the door located in the east. The northwest enjoys benevolent wealth luck. Money and opportunities come easily and are especially favorable this month for the family patriarch. Finances for him are good. Business will do well. If he intends to go into new business ventures, this is a good month to do so. The northeast is especially lucky because of the month star 8, so the time energy of the northeast is powerfully potent and positive, and also combines well with the natal chart numbers.

☆ MONTH 5: June 6–July 7

This month, luck takes a dive. Gossip, rumors, and bickering at work cause headaches and migraines, and there is also a great deal of tension and disagreement at home. The month 2 earth star causes these problems in conjunction with the annual star 5. In the southeast, luck is troublesome. Here the 3 star brings a great deal of disagreements and bickering - all very tiresome indeed. The northwest, meanwhile, plays host to the 5 yellow star this month so there is bad luck, obstacles, loss, and illness associated with the patriarch. It is definitely not a good month for him.

The northeast will enjoy a relatively good month, while residents of the southwest will find romance and marriage opportunities will smile on them. In fact, romance and income luck are good and women benefit from these auspicious star numbers.

☆ MONTH 6: July 7–August 8

The annual 5 meets the monthly 1 in the east and money luck is now favorable - much better than last month. Overall income luck benefits from some good sectors, although there are also some difficult sectors as well. For instance, in the southwest the month 9 exhausts the annual 4 wood star so the elements are not harmonious.

The northwest benefits from the entry of 4 into the palace, bringing good fortune for business and relationships. The northwest is also good for academic pursuits. Anything relating to writing will do extremely well. The west is afflicted with illness stars. Sickness can be emotional, mental, or physical. Move to another room! The northeast and north enjoy some brief fantastic money luck. There is success and happy occasions.

☆ MONTH 7: August 8–September 8

The stars of the northwest palace are likely to cause quarrels and conflicts among siblings and between the generations. This brings danger to children, so they should move out of the sector during this month. Do not risk harm or severe illness befalling them. The lucky sector is again the southwest, where there will be good news and cause for celebration for residents staying there. This means good relationship and romance luck, and note that where there's harmony, there's always wealth!

☆ MONTH 8: September 8–October 8

This is a very prosperous and lucky month for east 2/3 houses, due to the monthly 8 visiting the east palace. Money matters will take a turn for the better. Business opportunities abound. Residents in the southeast receive the most good luck this month. Business meetings are successful. Family reunions are harmonious. Expectant mothers will produce a wonderful baby. It is a good month to conceive. This is a month of good news. The luck of the northwest, however, takes a plunge this month. This time it affects the relationship between husband and wife. It also affects pregnant women, so they should sleep in another room. Alternatively, hang a metal windchime to reduce the evil influence of the combination of stars. The west will suffer more family arguments this month. Those in the southwest should be careful of knife-related injury.

☆ MONTH 9: October 8–November 7

There's a step backward for the east 2/3 house this month. This time the problem is a breakdown in communications, which leads to disharmony within the family. The 7 in the east combines most unfavorably with the 5 stars in the east sector. There is danger of violence leading to problems. There is also the real danger of robbery and break-ins, so you should step up security. The 7 has turned ugly and is showing its true nature because it is being forced to coexist with the 5.

The northwest will continue to enjoy good luck this month. Also, in matters of love, there is a need to exercise some caution. If you're in education, however, this month is great for you!

☆ MONTH 10: November 7–December 6

The lucky and unlucky sectors are the same as month one.

☆ MONTH 11: December 7–January 4, 2003

The lucky and unlucky sectors are the same as month two.

☆ MONTH 12: January 5–February 3, 2003

The lucky and unlucky sectors are the same as month three.

A West 1 House or Building

Facing 247.5 to 262.5 degrees

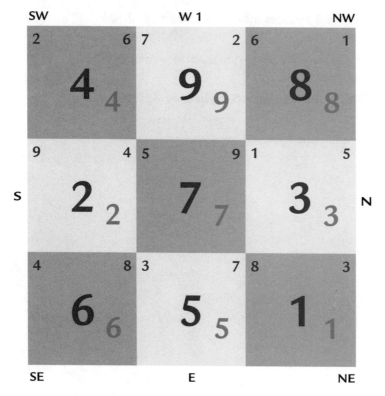

The natal chart for a **West 1** house in the year 2002 is shown on the left.

In the chart please note that the annual numbers in each grid are those in pink placed at the bottom right-hand corner.

The numbers in black represent the house natal chart. These numbers are also the period 7 numbers, and are referred to as the main numbers. The small numbers to the right of the main numbers are the water star numbers, while the small numbers on the left are the mountain star numbers.

General Outlook for the Year

Please note that the annual chart numbers are exactly the same as the period numbers in the year 2002. This is because the *Lo Shu* annual number for 2002 is 7, so the number 7 is also in the center grid. In a west 1-facing house, the numbers in the center of the grid show a 5/9 combination which, when combined with the double 7, tends to have its negative influences activated and even strengthened. Both the mountain and water stars are not very helpful at all. In this house it is excellent if there is a little room in the center of the house which can stay locked up so that the 5/9 combination is kept completely under wraps. This little room can be a storeroom or a toilet. If the dining room is here the natal numbers get energized, causing very troubled luck on a daily basis.

Note that the 7 is a most auspicious star in this period of 7, but the annual 7 holds different attributes to the natal 20-year 7 star, and although it is lucky in the natal chart, some of its intrinsic evil influence will emerge when it is the annual or monthly star. (In the period of 8, incidentally, the number 7 is deemed to be most unlucky.) So for west 1 houses, luck is simply not good this year because the annual 7 brings out the bad side of the 7 star and it is, of course, made worse by the 5 mountain star. As a result, there are going to be disappointments in relationships, which will deteriorate into very tiresome battles. It is going to be a rather unpleasant year. There is also the threat of robbery involving injury to limbs (getting hurt by metal or robbery). This is especially possible during the second and eleventh months (i.e. in March and December). In the fourth and seventh months (May and August), residents should also watch out for health hazards.

Wealth Luck

The annual 9 star enters the west, bringing fire strongly into a metal sector. This alone makes it a very trying year for residents of west 1-facing houses. This is because fire destroys metal. In addition, the combination of numbers in the natal chart also has the illness 2 star, which causes illness luck to ripen. Note also that a combination of 2 and 7 indicates hidden enemies working against you; so while luck appears good on the surface it is in effect not good at all. Children will also suffer illness and sleepless nights. The way to remedy this highly afflicted entrance palace is to place an urn filled with *yin* (still) water near the entrance. This will slow down the fire energy and also keep the earth energy under control. In general then, it is safest to view your wealth luck as being afflicted this year.

Meanwhile, at the back of the house in the east sector, residents have to cope with the full force of the 5 yellow annual star. Once again here is another indication that the wealth cycle of the house is seriously weakened this year. The natal mountain star is 3 and the natal water star is 7. So in the east the deadly 5 star saps the energy of the mountain star while corrupting the 7 star – in this sort of situation wealth luck has gone underground!

The 5 star entering into the east where the mountain star is 3 means there is loss of wealth, frequent quarrels, and many misunderstandings pertaining to money matters. So do be careful of loss of wealth arising from quarrels and litigations. And since the east palace is the palace at the back of the house, make sure you watch your back! Troubles emanate, unseen by you, and strike when you least expect them.

Good money luck is indicated in the southeast palace where the 8 water star is located. This is probably the luckiest sector of the house since the natal numbers, as well as the annual numbers, look promising. Build a waterfall in the garden at this corner of the house to stimulate good money luck. You need to do this because the rest of the house suggests poor money luck. Also, place a window or door in this palace to symbolically welcome in the money in the form of flowing water. Make very sure that the water is flowing in and not away from the house.

Health Luck

With the annual 5 in the east palace, health luck here deteriorates this year. Note that the mountain star in this sector is 7. Now the focus is on the 5 earth star coming in to a 7 mountain – this strengthens the mountain star but, as 5 is also a star that brings illness and bad news, the analysis here is that the 5 has caused the mountain star to turn negative. It is therefore not good for health. There will be physical discomfort as well as the possibility of surgery. Injury caused to the limbs is also a possibility.

The problem is serious, especially since the center grid has the 5/9 combination and the annual 7 is also in the center. So generally there are many indications that health luck is not good. It is wise to be careful. Do not overexert yourself and also do not take unnecessary risks with your health. Go for a medical checkup and have enough sleep. This is not a year to be adventurous.

Relationship Luck

The good news is that 2002 is favorable for those in love. The romantic 4 star number flies into the southwest, bringing opportunities for relationships between lovers to blossom into marriage. The love scene for those of you who are single during this year looks promising. This is especially true for the young women of the house. They stand a good chance of finding someone suitable to love, so there is romance luck of the serious kind. Those who are married will also enjoy good ties with their spouse. There is harmony and happiness.

The most promising palace for love is the southeast, where the mountain star 4 combines well with the water star 8. Those residing in the southeast will find their social and love life blossoming in total perfection. This analysis is based on the romantic star 4 being the mountain star. The mountain star governs relationships luck. At the same time, since 4 belongs to the wood element and is the original number of the southeast sector – all signs favor serious marriage luck ripening. Meanwhile, because the water star here is the very auspicious 8, money luck is also present. Finally, note the appearance of the 6 annual star here. The 6 star is bringing marriage luck from heaven. Since the southeast favors the daughters of the family, there are good indications of marriage possibilities in households with daughters of marriageable age.

Note that the northeast is also favorable as this sector has an auspicious mountain star 8, which brings excellent relationship luck to residents of this sector. The annual number 1 star flying in is also a good indication of smooth sailing, since water *chi* is strengthened thereby bringing good fortune.

Prosperous Palaces

The most prosperous sectors of this house during the year 2002, the year of the water horse, are the southeast and the northwest palaces. The southeast has the water star 8, while the northwest has a fantastic configuration of white stars (1, 6, and 8) and from a prosperity viewpoint these are the most auspicious stars of all. Any very lucky water star in any sector should always be activated if wealth luck is what you want!

As far as the southeast is concerned, since the luck of 6 means it comes from heaven, any good fortune experienced by those in the southeast sector will be very real and long lasting. Residents of this palace will experience excellent income luck, recognition, and fame during the year. There are honors from higher-ranking officials and help from influential people. Mentor luck just flows. Those in politics or business will be successful. Anything to do with gold and metal will succeed. There is an abundance of wealth luck. Health is also vibrant.

Meanwhile, the excellent configuration of stars in the northwest (especially the awesome annual 8 star) is strongly supported by the 1 water star. This highlights the strong influence of water, which brings prosperity and money luck. Those residing in this palace of the house will benefit strongly from the auspicious water star. It is an excellent idea to build a water feature that will activate the water star here.

When energized by water features, any palace that has an auspicious water star will always attract plenty of money luck. Both the luck sectors identified here have auspicious water stars. So in the southeast activate the auspicious 8 water star, and in the northwest (which is the luckiest sector this year with the annual 8 star) also activate the with the 1 water star a water feature.

Dangerous Palaces

All houses are affected by the deadly 5 yellow star, which in 2002 has flown to the east. Unfortunately the east also has the main star 5, and the combination of two 5s can, and usually does, have a deadly effect. This applies to all houses during the year, irrespective of their orientation. The effect of the Five Yellow is felt most in months two and eleven (i.e. in March and December), when the monthly 5 also comes visiting the east palace. Anyone with a bedroom located in the east is almost certain to succumb to some kind of illness. So the east is a dangerous palace this year.

The other sector to be wary of is the south sector, where the annual 2 star has flown in to combine with the 9 mountain star and the 4 water star. The 9/4 combination, especially in the south, suggests a certain danger from fire. Place an urn of *yin* (still) water here. It's best if the container is round.

Month-by-Month Analysis

☆ MONTH 1: February 4–March 6

In the first month the auspicious monthly 1 star enters the west palace. This brings money luck to the entrance sector but also creates an unstable combination with the 9 annual star, which suggests some small problems. The other lucky sectors of the house for this first month are the center and the east sectors of the house. In these sectors, the monthly stars are the auspicious 8 and the equally lucky 6. Residents in both sectors will have a fairly smooth time in their careers. There is some easy success this month, although luck is truly not spectacular.

The south palace is afflicted with the combination of 2/3 annual and monthly stars, bringing with it aggravation and heartaches. Residents in this sector should stay calm and practice some meditation, otherwise they will quarrel with everyone. Fire energy is also strong so some *yin* (still) water placed here should soothe frayed nerves. Meanwhile, the southwest is visited by the 5 star, which brings bad luck and loss. Romance for residents of this palace will turn stressful. Once again stay cool. When tough times hit at your relationship luck, nothing you do will improve it so it's better not to do very much.

☆ MONTH 2: March 6–April 5

In this month the auspicious locations are the northwest, the southeast, and the northeast. These three palaces are not part of the axis line of the house at all, which means that generally speaking the wealth luck of the home is not great. However, if bedrooms or important rooms are located in the auspicious palaces, wealth luck gets enhanced for those residing in those rooms.

So note that in the northwest, money and career luck are excellent. There is the suggestion that incomes will rise and there are prospects of promotion; some may even be lucky enough to gain windfall profits. Patriarch luck will also benefit. In any case, the northwest palace of this house has some powerful natal chart stars so this should be regarded as a very significant part of this house. Make very sure that your toilets and kitchens are not housed here. Otherwise the good luck of this house will simply be wasted.

The southeast has the double 6 flying into a sector where the water star is the powerful 8. The month's wealth luck for this sector is said to be excellent indeed, so if your room or office is located in this palace, you are on a roll! You can start to work out the numbers on any new investments you may be contemplating. Luck is on your side so go for it.

The northeast, meanwhile, enjoys the double 1 stars. This, too, brings in success and good energy as the mountain star here is the auspicious 8 star. The excellent monthly star will activate the luck of good and smooth relationships.

☆ MONTH 3: April 5–May 6

The wealth luck of the house continues to be strong this month as the auspicious prosperity and success star 8 enters the entrance palace of the house. This combines eloquently with the annual 9 star, causing there to be occasions for celebrations. Money continues to flow in but it is small money luck. However, all endeavors run smoothly.

At the back, in the east palace, the romantic star 4 flies in, bringing romance as well as some success in communications and interpersonal behavior. Here there is a need for restraint to be exercised when it comes to emotional matters. It is a month of the peach blossom when love blooms. Enjoy it by all means but do not go overboard as misunderstandings can arise, caused by the annual star 5. Never forget the pervasive impact of this horrible number. So here in the east, the 4 star brings love and even some career luck for those in advertising, publicity, and journalism – but stay wary. Hanging a six-rod windchime here should help you to keep the Five Yellow under control.

☆ MONTH 4: May 6–June 6

The ambivalent 7 star enters the west palace, combining rather unfortunately with the 9 annual star here. There is bad luck caused by sexual affairs. These emotional entanglements will drain residents of their vitality. Place big boulders tied with a red ribbon at the entrance to press down the bad luck being brought in by third parties. Residents living in the southeast palace will get involved in love entanglements that will also sap their energy but here, since the annual star is 6, heaven luck brings some help.

This month good luck enters the northeast and the northwest. If you have doors in these sectors use them. The northwest enjoys power and control this month. Those in authority will have their influence strengthened.

The northeast has personal advancement luck and those in leadership positions will benefit. Those in military or in physical occupations (sportspeople) will also enjoy a month of success. Those in high positions achieve recognition. Enhance with a mountain feature to take advantage of the mountain star 8, which is being strengthened this month by the monthly star 8 also having flown into the northeast.

☆ MONTH 5: June 6–July 7

Luck becomes frustrating this month as the 6 flies into the west, combining with the annual star 9 to bring a month of ups and downs and lots of arguments. At the same time, the east sector at the back of the house – which makes up the other end of the house axis line – has become decidedly afflicted. Here the combination of stars shows the dangerous 5/2 this month, bringing bad luck to the palace and to the axis.

It is vital to place some metal windchimes in the east this month to try and control the bad combination. Residents here will feel lethargic, and will succumb easily to common colds and temper tantrums. The northwest, meanwhile, houses the monthly 5, bringing sickness chi to the patriarch. June is therefore a difficult month for this house.

☆ MONTH 6: July 7–August 8

In this month the 5 star brings its negative *chi* to the west, where it combines with the 9 annual star. In terms of energy, this creates even more afflictions for the house than last month. This is because now it is the entrance palace that is being hurt by the 5 and, since the 9 strengthens it further, luck turns dangerous. Hang metallic six-rod windchimes here to control the 5 star. That this is already a metallic palace (the west is metal energy) does help matters somewhat. Nevertheless, strengthen the metal and make sure that the lights here are kept dim all through the month of July.

The lucky sector this month is the northeast, where the monthly 6 star combines auspiciously with the 1 annual star. The other lucky sector of the house this month is the northwest, where the monthly 4 also combines well with the annual 8 star. There is good fortune luck. Residents here will enjoy favorable energy this month.

☆ MONTH 7: August 8–September 8

The outlook for this month improves as the 4 star flies in to the west sector. This creates a combination that favors students, as well as those engaged in the communications business. Love luck is also good.

In the east, however, the monthly 9 star has flown in, thereby activating serious problems arising from the double 5 combination of this sector. Since the east is the back of the house, the negative impact affects all the residents. The remedy lies in hanging metal windchimes and placing lots of feng shui coins (those with the square hole in the center and preferably with the early heaven trigrams printed on one side of the coin) in this sector. A side effect of the problem of the number combination is that the young will challenge the older generation and that those in authority will face confrontation from subordinates. Household matters are in some disarray, while communication between parents and children is at a low ebb. This is a challenging month indeed.

☆ MONTH 8: September 8–October 8

The numbers continue to indicate tiresome problems this month. In the west, residents now have to cope with the hostile and quarrelsome 3 star. This creates tiresome vibrations, especially since the water star of the sector is also the unlucky 2 star. So in general this is not a good month. The only consolation is that the 8 star has flown to the east so that some hidden and unexpected good news could come to the house. Nevertheless, September will continue to be a challenging month for this house. Do not be surprised, also, if the patriarch of the house is taken ill and the matriarch becomes a victim of armed robbery.

☆ MONTH 9: October 8–November 7

Luck for this house still has not changed. In the ninth month, the illness star 2 enters the west entrance palace and combines with the annual 9 to bring huge sickness *chi* to the household. Last month the house had to face contentious quarrels; this month the household could succumb to very afflicted winds and waters that bring illness and lethargy.

At the same time, the 7 star has entered the east palace. Usually the 7 star is regarded as a lucky star in the present period of 7, nevertheless as a time dimension star for either the year or the month it is usually regarded as an evil star, especially when it combines with the 5, 2, or 9. In this case, the 7 combines with the 5 star in the east to bring the threat of robbery with violence. If you have a house with a west 1-facing door, you are said to be sitting in the east 1 location, so I strongly urge you to beef up on your security since the danger of break-ins and armed robbery is very real. Take extra precautions. Keep a dog as this will be a strong deterrent. Also hang windchimes in the east and place an inverted broom outside your main front door.

The lucky palaces this month are the southeast, with the monthly star 8 which brings good money luck; the northwest, which enjoys the monthly 1 star; and the southwest, which has the auspicious 6 star. All three sectors indicate good vibrations for their residents so that on balance, as long as proper precautions and remedies are taken to overcome the bad stars in the entrance, the luck of the household will hold up well to unfortunate entrance stars. To reduce their impact on the household, keep doors closed at all times. If you have doors in the lucky sectors of the home, use them rather than the doors in the afflicted sectors of east and west.

☆ MONTH 10: November 7–December 6

The lucky and unlucky sectors are the same as month one.

☆ MONTH 11: December 7–January 4, 2003

The lucky and unlucky sectors are the same as month two.

☆ MONTH 12: January 5–February 3, 2003

The lucky and unlucky sectors are the same as month three.

A West 2 or 3 House or Building

Facing 262.5 to 292.5 degrees

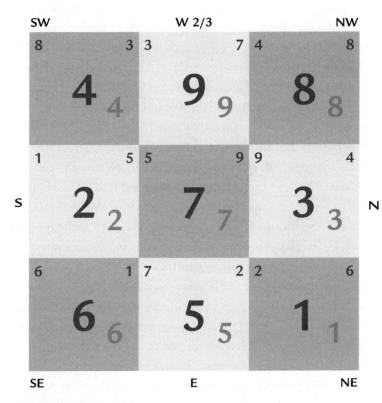

The natal chart for a **West 2 or 3** house in the year 2002 is shown on the left.

In the chart please note that the annual numbers in each grid are those in pink placed at the bottom right-hand corner.

The numbers in black represent the house natal chart. These numbers are also the period 7 numbers, and are referred to as the main numbers. The small numbers to the right of the main numbers are the water star numbers, while the small numbers on the left are the mountain star numbers.

General Outlook for the Year

Please note that the annual chart numbers are exactly the same as the period numbers in the year 2002. This is because the *Lo Shu* annual number for 2002 is 7, so the number 7 is also in the center grid. In a west 2/3-facing house the numbers in the center of the grid show a 5/9 combination which, when combined with the double 7, tends to have its negative influences activated and even strengthened. Both the mountain and water stars are not helpful. In this house it will be excellent if there is a small room in the center of the house, which can stay locked up so that the 5/9 combination is kept completely under wraps. This can be a storeroom or a toilet. If there is a dining room here the natal numbers get energized daily, causing luck to be very troubled indeed.

Note that the 7 is usually an auspicious star in this period of 7. However, the annual 7 holds different attributes to the natal 20-year 7 star and although it is lucky in the natal chart, some of its intrinsic evil influence will emerge when it is the annual or monthly star. (By the way, in the coming period of 8, the number 7 is deemed to be very unlucky.) So for west 2/3 houses, luck does not look very promising this year because the annual 7 brings out the bad side of the 7 star in the center and it is, of course, made worse by the 5 mountain star. This looks like a rather unpleasant year.

There is also the threat of robbery involving injury to limbs (possibly being hurt by metal). This is because of the mountain/water star combination at the entrance palace, which is 3 and 7 respectively. This combination indicates robbery and burglary, so violence is a possibility as is serious injury. This is especially possible during the second and eleventh months (i.e. in March and December), so please take very stringent precautions. What are the remedies? Try not to use the west-facing door, place urns of water near the west-facing door, and keep the west very quiet during the months of March and December. Also, keep the front door area well lit. Fire energy will dissipate the evil influence of the number 7. Keep the lights turned on all night! Please do not take this warning lightly. Perhaps this is why your karma led you to pick up this book – to bring your attention to some of the afflicted energies that surround your house. Prevention is always better than cure, so take note of the danger months in the year!

Wealth Luck

The annual 9 star enters the west, bringing strong fire into this metal sector. This generally suggests a year of conflict and difficulty for residents of west-facing houses. This is because fire destroys metal. In addition, the combination of numbers in the natal chart also has the 3/7 combination of mountain and water stars in the entrance palace, and this is a clear indication of getting injured in an armed robbery. There is also the danger that violence will be the result and injury is caused by metal i.e. guns and knives. There is no wealth luck indicated. Instead what is shown is that there could be a loss of wealth.

Meanwhile, at the back of the house, in the east sector, residents have to cope with the full force of the 5 yellow annual star. Once again here is another indication that the wealth cycle of the house is seriously bad this year. The natal mountain star is 7 and the natal water star is 2. So in the east the deadly 5 star corrupts the energy of the mountain star, while combining with the 2 water star to bring about intense bad luck and misfortunes.

The situation in a west 2/3 house is worse than that of the west 1 house.

With the 5 star entering into the east, loss of wealth, quarrels, and misunderstandings pertaining to money matters are all indicated. You must be careful of loss of wealth arising from quarrels and litigation. And since the east palace is the palace at the back of the house make sure you also watch your back! Robbers could come to your home and carry your wealth away.

Some money luck, however, is indicated in the northwest palace, where the 8 water star is located. This is also the sector where the annual star 8 resides, so this is probably the luckiest sector of the house since the natal numbers, as well as the annual numbers, look promising. Build a waterfall in the garden at this corner of the house to stimulate good money luck. You need to do this because the rest of the house suggests very afflicted luck this year. Also place a window or door here to symbolically welcome in the money in the form of flowing water. Make very sure that the water is flowing in and not away from the house. This is one excellent way to overcome the misfortunes of the year. If there is a door here, use it as often as you can. This will activate the auspicious *chi* that resides in this corner of the house.

Health Luck

With the annual 5 in the east palace, the health luck of this house deteriorates this year since the east is the sitting direction of the house.

Note that the mountain star in this sector is 7. Now the focus is on the 5 earth star coming in to a 7 mountain – this strengthens the mountain star but, because 5 is also a star that brings illness and bad news, the analysis here is that the 5 has caused the mountain star to turn negative, and it is therefore not good for health. There will be physical discomfort, as well as the possibility of surgery. Injury caused to the limbs is also a possibility. In addition, the water star here is the illness star 2 – hence afflicted health is strongly indicated.

The problem is serious, especially as the center grid has the 5/9 combination and the annual 7 is also in the center. These are indications that health luck is generally not good, so it is wise to be careful. Do not over exert yourself and also do not take unnecessary risks. Go for a medical checkup and ensure you have enough sleep. This is not a year to be adventurous.

In addition, the south palace is also very seriously affected by the annual 2 star which in turn combines with the 5 water star there. Since the south is a fire sector, this indicates that the 2s and the 5 are strengthened by the fire, making them even more dangerous. Hang windchimes here and take care not to allow pregnant women or nursing mothers to sleep here. Children should also be moved out of the east and south palaces of the home.

Relationship Luck

Relationship luck in 2002 is somewhat mixed for those in love. The romantic 4 star flies into the southwest, bringing luck for lovers who are looking to get married. The love scene for those of you who are single during this year looks promising. Unfortunately, in the southwest, although the mountain star is the very auspicious 8 star (thereby bringing depth to love relationships), lovers will still have to contend with the quarrelsome 3 water star. This suggests misunderstandings over money, careers, and other mundane issues that have to do with the realities of living. Those wanting their love life to stay smooth should consider placing six round and smooth crystal balls in the southwest. They can be of any size but they should be made of natural quartz crystal so that the earth energy is strong and can support the romantic 4 annual star. Do not place water, as this causes the 4 to turn scandalous.

In a west 2/3 house the most promising palace for relationship luck to blossom is the northwest, where the mountain star 4 combines well with the water star 8. Those residing here will find their love life blossoming nicely. The mountain star governs relationship luck and the 4 is considered auspicious for this purpose. Meanwhile, because the water star here is also very auspicious, being the 8, money luck is also present. Finally, most telling of all, note the appearance of the 8 annual star here. The 8 star is bringing good fortune luck from heaven.

Prosperous Palaces

The most prosperous sectors of this house during the year 2002, the year of the water horse, are the northwest and southeast palaces. The northwest has the water star 8, while the southeast has the favorable *ho tu* configuration of white stars (1 and 6), and from a prosperity viewpoint these are very auspicious stars. Lucky water stars in any sector should always be activated with the presence of a water feature if wealth luck is what you want.

In the northwest (especially with the awesome annual 8 star), the 8 water star is strongly supported by the 4 mountain star. Those residing in this palace of the house will benefit strongly from the auspicious water star. It is an excellent idea to build a water feature that will activate the water star here.

As far as the southeast is concerned, since the luck of 6 means it comes from heaven, any good fortune experienced by those in the southeast sector will be very real and long lasting. Those residing in this palace will experience excellent income luck, wealth, and prosperity during the year. Once again, placing a *yang* (bubbling) water feature in this part of the house will create strong money luck.

Dangerous Palaces

All houses are affected by the deadly 5 yellow star, which in 2002 has flown to the east. Unfortunately the east also has the main star 5, and the combination of two 5s can, and usually does, have a deadly effect. This applies to all houses during the year without exception. The effect of the Five Yellow is felt most in months two and eleven (i.e. in March and December), when the monthly 5 also come visiting the east palace. Anyone whose bedroom is located in the east is almost certain to succumb to some kind of illness. So the east is a dangerous palace this year. Either move out of the room or, if this is not possible, hang plenty of six-rod metal windchimes. The other sector to be wary of is the south sector where the annual 2 star has flown in to combine with the 5 water star. The 1/5 combination in the natal chart suggests danger from recurring health problems caused by food poisoning and by accidents. There is also affliction to the kidneys. Make sure you have a proper medical checkup if you reside in the south palace of your home.

Month-by-Month Analysis

☆ MONTH 1: February 4–March 6

In the first month the auspicious monthly 1 star enters the west palace, bringing money luck to the entrance sector. Unfortunately it also creates an unstable combination with the 9 annual star, which activates the negative impact of the 3/7 combination in the natal chart. Place an urn of water in the entrance to reduce the possibility of burglary. The 8 star visits the center of the house, and in the east the auspicious 6 star flies into the sector. This brings benefits to residents, who thus enjoy some easy success in their careers this month. However, luck is not spectacular because the natal chart numbers are not particularly special.

In the south palace, serious problems will be caused by the combination of the 2/3 annual and monthly stars, bringing with them aggravation and heartaches. Residents in this sector have to endure a spate of bad luck, which manifests itself in illness and accidents. Truly the combination of the natal chart and the annual stars in this palace is quite horrendous –

with plenty of 2s and 5s. This is a classical case of bad feng shui and residents are strongly advised to keep any room in the south closed and unused through the year, starting from this month.

Meanwhile, the southwest is visited by the 5 star, which brings bad luck and loss to the women of the household. Relationships between spouses become stressful and unhappy. Once again stay cool. When tough times hit at your relationship luck, nothing you do will look right so it's better not to do very much. To reduce the impact of the 5 star, hang a six-rod metal windchime.

☆ MONTH 2: March 6–April 5

The northwest benefits from the auspicious double 8 stars and since the water star is also 8, money and career luck are excellent for the patriarch and for all residents residing in this part of the house. Income will increase and there are many opportunities at work for growth and upward mobility. Make very sure that your toilets and kitchens are not housed here, otherwise the good luck of this house will simply be wasted. And to tap strongly into the powerful configuration of 8s in this palace, do build a water feature here.

The southeast is also auspicious this month. Here the double 6 stars match brilliantly with the 1 water star. There is plenty of wealth luck in this palace and good money flows inward. In the northeast the annual stars and water star are also auspicious.

☆ MONTH 3: April 5–May 6

The entrance palace benefits from the 8 monthly star. This brings wealth luck into the home and combines powerfully with the annual 9 star, creating auspicious occasions for celebrations. Money flows in but it is small money luck. Nevertheless, all endeavors go smoothly.

The east palace benefits from the auspicious and romantic star 4, which brings romance luck as well as success for those engaged in the writing professions and those in college or at school.

☆ MONTH 4: May 6–June 6

In the fourth month, problems are caused by sexual entanglements. Note that the ambivalent 7 star enters the west palace, combining rather unfortunately with the 9 annual star here. There is bad luck in money matters that is caused by illicit romantic affairs. Residents should beware of emotional entanglements that will drain them of their vitality.

To press down the bad luck being brought in by outside third parties, place big boulders tied with a red ribbon at the entrance. Residents living in the southeast palace will see themselves getting involved in love entanglements that will also sap their energy, but here the annual star is 6, so heaven luck brings some help. Also, the natal chart stars here are auspicious so that there should be no problem for residents of this sector.

☆ MONTH 5: June 6–July 7

Luck becomes a frustrating exercise this month as the 6 flies into the west to combine with the annual star 9, bringing a frustrating month of ups and downs and lots of arguments. At the same time the east sector at the back of the house, which makes up the other end of the house axis line, has become decidedly afflicted. Here the combination of stars shows the dangerous 5/2 this month, bringing bad luck to the palace and to the axis.

It is vital to place some metal windchimes in the east this month to try and control the bad combination. Residents here will feel lethargic and will be lacking in vitality. They succumb easily to common colds and temper tantrums. The northwest, meanwhile, houses the monthly 5, bringing sickness *chi* to the patriarch. June seems to be a most difficult month for this house.

☆ MONTH 6: July 7–August 8

In this month the 5 star brings its negative *chi* to the west, where it combines with the 9 annual star. In terms of energy, this creates even more afflictions for the house than last month. This is because it is the entrance palace that is now being hurt by the 5 and since the 9 strengthens it further, luck turns dangerous. Hang six-rod metallic windchimes here to control the 5 star. Note that the west is already a metallic palace (the west is metal energy) and this does help matters somewhat. Nevertheless, strengthen the metal and make sure that the lights here are kept dim all through the month of July.

The lucky sector this month is the northeast, where the 6 monthly star combines auspiciously with the 6 water star and the 1 annual star. This is the excellent early heaven *ho tu* combination which brings a window of real wealth luck to residents of this house. If you have a door in this part of the house, use it this month to activate the good *chi* of this sector.

The other lucky sector of the house this month is the northwest, where the monthly 4 combines well with the annual 8 star. There is good fortune luck. Residents here will enjoy favorable energy this month. Remember that the water star 8 is placed in the northwest, so this is a powerfully auspicious corner. Try to tap this corner as much as you can as it has the potential to overcome the bad luck associated with the house axis line.

☆ MONTH 7: August 8–September 8

The outlook for this month improves as the 4 star flies in to the west sector. This creates a combination that favors students, as well as those engaged in the communications business. Love luck is also good.

In the east, however, the monthly 9 star has flown in, thereby activating serious problems arising from the double 5 combination of this sector. Since the east is the back sitting direction of the house, the negative impact affects all the residents of the household. The remedy lies in hanging metal windchimes and placing lots of feng shui coins (those with the square hole in the center and preferably those with the early heaven trigrams printed on one side of the coin) in this sector.

A side effect of the problem of the number combination is that the young will challenge the older generation and those in authority will face confrontation from subordinates. Household matters are in some disarray, while communication between parents and children is at a low ebb. This is challenging month indeed.

✭ MONTH 8: September 8–October 8

The numbers continue to indicate tiresome problems this month. In the west, residents now have to cope with the hostile and quarrelsome 3 star. This creates very severe quarrelsome vibes for the sector, and for the house in general because the mountain star of the palace (which governs relationships) is also the hostile 3 star. With the gathering of 3s in this palace this month, misunderstandings have the potential to turn ugly and contentious. The result could even turn violent, since we also have the 9 as the annual star and the 7 as the water star in this palace. The only consolation is that the 8 star has flown to the east so there could be some unexpected good news coming to the house. Nevertheless, September continues to be a very challenging month for this house. Do not be surprised also if the patriarch of the house is taken ill and the matriarch becomes a victim of armed robbery.

✭ MONTH 9: October 8–November 7

The luck of the house continues to remain rather tiresome. Note that the illness star 2 now enters the west entrance palace, combining with the annual 9 to manifest big sickness *chi*. Last month the house had to face contentious quarrels; this month the household could succumb to very afflicted winds and waters that bring sickness and despondency. It certainly does not look good at all.

Meanwhile, the 7 month star has entered the east palace. Usually the 7 star is regarded as a lucky star in the present period of 7, nevertheless as a time dimension star for either the year or the month it is usually regarded as an evil star, especially when it combines with the 5, the 2, or the 9. In this case, the 7 combines with the 5 star in the east. The effect is to bring the threat of robbery with violence into the picture. If you have a house with a west 1 facing door you are said to be sitting in the east 1 location, so I strongly urge you to beef up on your security since the danger of break-ins and armed robbery is very real. Take extra precautions. Keep a dog as this will be a strong deterrent. Also hang windchimes in the east and place an inverted broom outside your main front door.

The lucky palaces this month are the southeast with the monthly star 8, which brings good money luck; the northwest, which enjoys the monthly 1 star; and the southwest palace, which has the auspicious 6 star. All three sectors indicate good vibrations for their residents so on balance, as long as proper precautions and remedies are taken to overcome the bad stars in the entrance, the luck of the household can hold up well to the unfortunate stars plaguing the axis line of the house.

To reduce the impact on the household of the inauspicious numbers of the entrance palace, keep doors closed at all times. If you have doors in the lucky sectors of the home use them, rather than the afflicted doors in the afflicted sectors of east and west. Better yet, if it is possible make new entrance doors in the northwest sector, which is generally regarded as being very lucky this year.

☆ MONTH 10: November 7–December 6

The lucky and unlucky sectors are the same as month one.

☆ MONTH 11: December 7–January 4, 2003

The lucky and unlucky sectors are the same as month two.

☆ MONTH 12: January 5–February 3, 2003

The lucky and unlucky sectors are the same as month three.

2002

A Southeast 1 House or Building

Facing 112.5 to 127.5 degrees

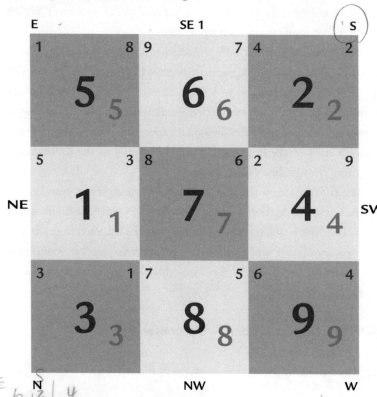

The natal chart for a **Southeast 1** house in the year 2002 is shown on the left.

In the chart please note that the annual numbers in each grid are those in pink placed at the bottom right-hand corner.

The numbers in black represent the house natal chart. These numbers are also the period 7 numbers, and are referred to as the main numbers. The small numbers to the right of the main numbers are the water star numbers, while the small numbers on the left are the mountain star numbers.

General Outlook for the Year

Please note that the annual chart numbers are exactly the same as the period numbers in the year 2002. This is because the *Lo Shu* annual number for 2002 is 7, so the number 7 is also in the center grid. In a southeast 1-facing house the numbers in the center of the grid show an auspicious 8/6 combination which, when combined with the double 7, has an enhancing effect on the excellent outlook for the house or building. If this house has an "open" center – which means there is no small room in the center of the home imprisoning the auspicious configuration of numbers – then the entire household will benefit from the good energy.

The year of the water horse brings strong heaven luck to this house. This comes from the incidence of the double 6 auspicious star flying in to the southeast sector this year. By entering the southeast palace, the 6 star brings good *chi* and prosperity to the residents. However, this is a wood sector and, since 6 is a metal number, there is a disharmony of elements. Also, the 6 and 7 combination reflected in the annual star's effect on the water star is that of "sword fighting killing breath." So while there is prosperity luck, there is also a great deal of anger and disagreement. The energy is disturbing and unstable, rather than calm and smooth. This clash of elements is energized if the front door of the house is actually located in the southeast palace. This is because activity caused by the use of the door will further aggravate the tension, and instability will grow. The result is that, while good fortune comes to the house, residents will be unable to take advantage of these opportunities without quarrelling.

A house with a southeast 1 orientation does not have very good natal chart numbers in its SE/NW axis, apart from the 7 water star in the southeast and the 7 mountain star in the northwest. This water and mountain star combination in the front and back palaces will become less and less fortunate as we get nearer to 2004, when the period changes to period 8. The 7 star is already waning and transforming from good to bad so that soon the 7, instead of bringing wealth luck, will become less and less fortunate. However, in the year 2002 the annual numbers for these two sectors – being 6 in the southeast and 8 in the northwest – are excellent. What this does is to activate the main *Lo Shu* numbers in these palaces, thereby improving the luck of the house considerably during the year. It also brings supporting energy to the 7 stars so that luck is still good. However, households with this natal chart should be starting to think of the changeover of period.

Wealth Luck

Wealth luck is quite good for this house because the annual star 8 enters the northwest, thereby benefiting the breadwinner/patriarch's luck. If the patriarch is residing in the south, however, this luck is not so good since the south is seriously afflicted by the 2 star, which brings illness.

The east palace has the auspicious 8 water star and the 1 mountain star – a good natal chart positioning. However, the *Lo Shu* number is 5 and in 2002 the annual number is also 5. This causes wealth luck to become seriously afflicted. Place plenty of windchimes in the east to overcome the effect of the Five Yellow and to protect your wealth luck.

Health Luck

The annual 5 enters the east palace where there is an 8 water star, thereby afflicting it. The annual 2 star, meanwhile, enters the south and this combines with the 2 Lo Shu number and the 2 water star to bring very severe illness luck to the daughters of the household. If your bedroom is also located in this palace you will get sick and it could be fatal. Those staying in the south will feel weak and lethargic this year. So in terms of health, the east and south are not good.

All other parts of the home, however, are fine and this is due to the auspicious numbers in the center grid of the house. Here there is a beautiful combination and residents will therefore enjoy a vibrant and healthy lifestyle. You will find yourself working out at the gym and playing sports extremely well. Golfers benefit from their daily exercise rounds, and tennis addicts will feel the benefits of their fitness regime. Major illnesses are unlikely and those with long-term illness will see improvements in their condition this year. Just avoid sleeping in the east and south. The north is also not the best place for health but it is nevertheless benefiting from the good water star 1.

Relationship Luck

Romantic involvements are likely for young men and women residing in the southwest of the house, and happy occasions revolving around the family and the success of the womenfolk will take place this year.

Remember that it is an excellent year for getting married, so those with plans to do so can proceed with confidence. In fact, weddings and engagements will lead to long-term happiness and those who are already married will discover each other again. Husband and wife will enjoy very good relations with each other. To make certain all these good indications do manifest themselves, it is a good idea to hang a six-rod windchime discreetly on the wall of this palace. This is to take care of the afflicted mountain star 2 here.

Prosperous Palaces

The southeast 1 house has a water star 7 in the southeast palace and this is a good indication. And since the prosperous 6 stars are also there, the sector enjoys good luck. However, it is also necessary to consider that the 7 star is waning, since period 7 is coming to a close.

The east palace of the house or building will also enjoy good fortune and prosperity luck. In fact, this is the second best location and money luck is extremely strong. Careers will soar to great heights, as will income. But to attain this, residents will have to put up with a great deal of stress and high pressure. Success is achieved but it will not be without a cost. As they say, the road to success is paved with bumps and rocks, but the end result is worth everything! All this is due to the affliction caused by the annual 5 star having entered this palace this year. So anyone with his or her room or office located here will suffer some setbacks.

The other sector that is good for money is the northwest. The most auspicious 8 annual star serves this sector. If you wish to amass more power and authority this is the sector for you. It is an excellent room for those who are in the political field. Promotions will be possible this year, but these higher levels of authority do not necessarily come with pay increases. Note the water star 5 is not auspicious.

Dangerous Palaces

All houses are affected by the 5 yellow star, which in 2002 has flown to the east. Unfortunately the east also has the main star 5, and the combination of two 5s can, and usually does, have a deadly effect. This applies to all houses during the year, irrespective of their orientation. The effect of the Five Yellow is felt most in months two and eleven (i.e. in March and December), when the monthly 5 also comes visiting the east palace. Anyone with a bedroom located in the east will be certain to succumb to illness. Keep fresh flowers in the east to strengthen its intrinsic element *chi* of wood, since this has the power to control the Five Yellow.

The danger area in a southeast 1 house this year is where the annual 5 yellow star resides, which is east. With the annual 5 star bringing negative vibes, illness and loss is likely. To control this, use six-rod windchimes to exhaust the earth *chi* of the Five Yellow.

The south is also very afflicted this year. With the sickness star 2 causing financial problems (4 combining with lots of 2s), it is likely that those staying here will suffer money shortage, as well as illness and a tarnished reputation.

The north, with the annual 3 star, activates the inherently hostile 3 mountain star of the natal chart, thereby creating distress and more relationship problems. Residents who usually suffer from ill temper and impatience must move out of the north palace, otherwise their temper tantrums could cause them to get into severe hot water.

Month-by-Month Analysis

☆ MONTH 1: February 4–March 6

The auspicious monthly 7 star enters the southeast bringing monetary gains, success, and good fortune. Wealth luck is not at its peak, but it is considered to be a very good month and residents can invest with a certain confidence.

The lucky sectors of the house are in the center, in the east, and in the west, where all the good numbers 1, 6, and 8 reside this month. In the center the auspicious 8 star brings overall money luck to the whole house, unless it happens to have got locked away inside a small storeroom or toilet in the center. In the east the 6 brings good heavenly luck, while in the west the white star 1 brings good fortune. However, all this good fortune is rather modest, so it is still a good idea to be prudent. The month 9 star visits the northwest sector and, with an annual 8 in the *Chien* palace, this indicates that good luck in the northwest is enhanced. There will be cause for a few happy family celebrations.

☆ MONTH 2: March 6–April 5

This month the 6 enters the southeast. This has a positive effect on the residents' heaven luck because the 6 brings harmony and success. The 6 is an auspicious white star which brings heavenly luck, especially for the patriarch of the family. This indication is further strengthened by the 8 star having flown into the northwest, where it combines with the 8 annual star to bring awesome good fortune to residents of the northwest. You must activate this sector with lights and moving objects. It also helps if you make plenty of noise in this sector this month.

☆ MONTH 3: April 5–May 6

The luck cycle of the house declines this month. The inauspicious 5 star enters the southeast, instantly activating the sickness and accident *chi* and afflicting the 7 water star. Career and business prospects are thus not promising this month. This is an excellent time to lay low and quietly re-organize your thoughts, plans, and strategies so that you will be well poised to take advantage when the luck changes. Undertaking preparation this month will sow the right seeds because in the coming few months luck will turn auspicious and you can then reap huge rewards. At the same time, the north is seriously afflicted by the 2 star, which combines with the hostile star 3, thereby bringing a lot of quarrelsome energy into the household. It is a good idea to keep any room in the north sector closed this month in order to isolate the bad combination of stars. In this month, the northwest benefits from the 7 star and in the west the 8 star brings good news for residents there.

☆ MONTH 4: May 6–June 6

When the lucky 4 enters its original palace, i.e. the southeast, it exerts a very strong and very good influence. There is plenty of excellent relationship and growth luck this month for this palace, as well as for the entire household. Wealth luck is not at its peak, but it is considered to be a good month and definitely better than the previous month. Love matters also improve this month. There is a good chance for marriage.

Good luck continues in the northwest palace where the 6 white star now combines with the auspicious 8 annual star to bring good fortune. The wealth cycle moves up. There is acceptance of your position and authority, and you will emerge victorious in whatever project you are presently advancing. Status, fame, and success are likely and investments are good.

There are a lot of headaches for southwest residents and illness also impedes progress.

☆ MONTH 5: June 6–July 7

The quarrelsome star 3 enters the southeast and problems with verbal entanglements disturb the peace of your household. Stay away from romantic affairs as any attachment you form will not be beneficial. In fact, it could cause scandals to erupt all around you and gossiping will bring you down. The 3 causes setbacks in relationships and this is made worse by the 1 month star having flown into the southwest to combine with the 4 star. This combination always brings with it the danger of sexual scandals. So do not make hasty decisions on love affairs and note that it is not advisable to get married this month. Children in this house may get injured easily this month. Please take extra care of them.

The auspicious locations this month are the south and northeast sectors. Wealth and career luck are good in these sectors. Those in the south may receive windfall profits or enjoy a promotion. Northeast residents enjoy a month of great recognition luck which augurs well for their careers and their achievements. There are signs of promotion and increased income.

✬ MONTH 6: July 7–August 8

In the sixth month the horrible illness star 2 enters into the southeast palace, the entrance palace of this house, bringing illness and all sorts of lethargy and dullness. It debilitates the good stars of the palace. However, the saving grace is that since 2 is earth, it enhances the annual 6 star, which is metal, so although the 2 brings lethargy, it also strengthens the heavenly star 6.

The 8 star has flown to the north, bringing a spurt of good fortune to residents of this part of the house. The northwest enjoys the auspicious 4 star, which brings success as well as happiness in love. The southwest also has good luck this month.

✬ MONTH 7: August 8–September 8

This month the lucky 1 enters the southeast. The 1 star is a benevolent force and it brings auspicious wealth luck. Those working in the communications field will prosper and attain recognition. Fame and fortune are indicated. The luck cycle moves upward very quickly, so stop daydreaming and start harnessing opportunities that come by. Those embarking on a new course of study will do well this month. You should start setting yourself a goal. With the auspicious monthly 1 star, goals become easy to achieve.

Good luck also enters the south and southwest. The south has the power luck cycle this month. Those in authority will have their power and influence increased – subordinates and colleagues succumb to your wishes. However, the texts warn against arrogance and imply that humility brings greatness. The southwest will see improvements in financial standing. Those in earth element businesses will prosper. If you have a door in these sectors of your southeast 1 house and you use it, success and achievements will be awesome this month.

☆ MONTH 8: September 8–October 8

The cycle stabilizes this month. Those in high and authoritative positions will see their luck wane a little but career professionals will benefit from excellent relationship luck. Wealth luck will be good for those in the east palace, brought by the prosperous 8 star, but those residing in the northwest have to suffer through a month of the 2 illness star.

The south suffers setbacks this month. Trivial matters will drive you crazy. Be careful of your friends or employees sabortaging you behind your back through idle gossip. They could be the cause of many problems relating to money. Embezzlement and swindling of money within the company can be expected so be alert. In fact, your reputation could suffer this month as a result of the affliction to the south sector.

☆ MONTH 9: October 8–November 7

The month 8 star enters the southeast and wow! This is very auspicious. This is the best month of the year for the house. There is success in everything: achievements in real estate and property businesses, investments reap handsome returns, income flows in from various sources, and smooth sailing in business ventures. In addition, married couples yearning for a child will find this a very auspicious month to conceive. Your child will be intelligent and bright. Single people in southeast rooms will have marriage opportunities.

The dangerous sector, which is badly afflicted, is the north. The 5 may cause life-threatening accidents or situations. Please take serious precautions. Forget about remedying this sector; just get out of this room at once! No excuse! Don't take the risk. The west sector is very sickly this month because this sector has inherently bad natal stars.

☆ MONTH 10: November 7–December 6

The lucky and unlucky sectors are the same as month one.

☆ MONTH 11: December 7–January 4, 2003

The auspicious and unlucky sectors are the same as month two.

☆ MONTH 12: January 5–February 3, 2003

The lucky and unlucky sectors are the same as month three.

A Southeast 2 or 3 House or Building

Facing 127.5 to 157.5 degrees

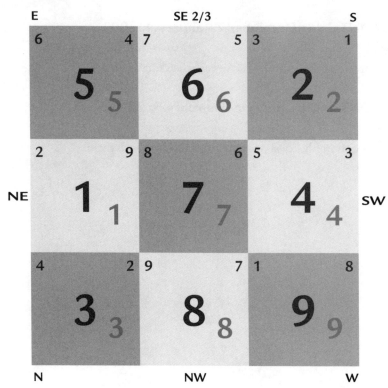

The natal chart for a **Southeast 2 or 3** house in the year 2002 is shown on the left.

In the chart please note that the annual numbers in each grid are those in pink placed at the bottom right-hand corner.

The numbers in black represent the house natal chart. These are also the period 7 numbers, and are referred to as the main numbers. The small numbers to the right of the main numbers are the water star numbers, while the small numbers on the left are the mountain star numbers.

General Outlook for the Year

Please note that the annual chart numbers are exactly the same as the period numbers in the year 2002. This is because the *Lo Shu* annual number for 2002 is 7, so the number 7 is also in the center grid. In a southeast 2/3-facing house the numbers in the center of the grid show an auspicious 8/6 combination which, when combined with the double 7, has an enhancing effect on the excellent outlook for the house or building. If this house has an "open" center – which means there is no small room in the center of the home imprisoning the auspicious configuration of numbers – then the entire household will benefit from the good energy.

This year, the auspicious annual 6 enters the southeast palace. The 6 star is generally considered to be a very lucky star which brings success and blessings from heaven. It brings power, influence, and authority when it enters your house, especially if you also have the front door located in the southeast palace. For southeast 2/3 houses, the wealth luck cycle is not as favorable as that of a southeast 1 house, but the luck this year is definitely better than last year. The auspicious 6 star enters the southeast and reduces the evil influence of the water star 5.

This year, residents will start to see improvements in their career and business. To maximize the luck of your southeast 2/3 orientation house, try to always use the back door – this means a door in the northwest palace. This is because generally the northwest enjoys the best fortunes this year and also the northwest palace of your home has an auspicious combination of star numbers.

If residents can enter though the northwest sector at the back of the house, their good fortune luck will multiply tenfold and they will enjoy tremendous success during the year. Otherwise, wealth luck will be just above average.

Wealth Luck

With the annual 6 entering the southeast, good luck comes to the house. The house is very favorable for long-term investment in real estate (earth-based related). If the door is in the south sector of the house, then wealth luck will be much better this year. Even if the door is in the east sector, the luck will be very good.

The luckiest palace in terms of wealth luck is definitely the northwest, which is blessed with the water star 7 (although the influence of 7 is now waning as the 7 period comes to a close in 2004). Nevertheless, the northwest can be tapped for money luck, especially with the combination of the double 8 period *Lo Shu* and annual 8. Another wealth palace is the west, where the water star 8 is located. This is enhanced by the presence of the double 9 *Lo Shu* and the annual stars. Build a water feature here to tap this water star for greater wealth luck this year. If your door is in the southeast, luck is just slightly better than last year. Smooth sailing yes, extravagant good luck definitely not. So consider changing the door you use.

Health Luck

In terms of health, this year is not at all bad. Residents of this house will enjoy a healthy lifestyle, although there is evidence of quick tempers and angry *chi*. The good luck is due mainly to the annual 6 and 8 stars entering the house axis line palaces of southeast and northwest. Note, however, that the entrance palace (southeast) has a mountain 7 star. The combination here of the 7 mountain star with an annual 6 star indicates anger and fighting tempers, so placing some *yin* (still) water here should calm tempers and allow the auspicious *chi* to flow.

The south palace is most afflicted this year with the illness star 2, which becomes really dangerous in months two and eleven (i.e. March and December). During these months, all residents who usually stay in the south are advised to sleep in another room as the threat of illness is extremely strong.

Relationship Luck

This is a year when young people living in a southeast 2/3 house will very likely meet their future spouse. Chances of a romance flowering into eventual marriage are indicated. Thus meetings of young men and women hold great promise.

Those who have just come out of a bad relationship can take things slowly and be assured that this is the time to unload last year's problems from their shoulders. This year is the time when feelings will be healed. Although there will be some slight entanglements, any new relationship this year will eventually have a happy ending. All these good vibes for romance and marriage come from the double 4 combination seen in the palace of the southwest, which governs these matters. In addition, the center palace has a most auspicious mountain star 8, which also helps relationship luck take control.

Prosperous Palaces

The best and luckiest location in a southeast 2/3 oriented house is the northwest palace. Here the water star 7 is strongly supported by the annual 8 star and the key words are power, status, authority, and wealth. So all you ambitious up-and-coming executives, managers, and businessmen residing in this area of the house can take heart from the knowledge that you will do well this year. The most auspicious time for wealth creation this year will be in the second and eleventh months.

The west sector is also supposed to be a lucky part of the house due to the presence of the water star 8, and this year it is strongly supported by the annual 9 star which has a multiplying effect, so the energy of the water star is deemed to be strong.

In the northeast, career luck will be strong and will soar to great heights and so will your income. However, to attain this upward ascendancy, ambitious residents here will need to overcome obstacles, and experience a great deal of stress. The problems are caused by hostilities and jealousies encountered at work, and issues related to their personal love life. So although luck may be good, the mountain star 2 and the water star 9 complicate life. It can be said that the natal chart is not promising but the annual and *Lo Shu* main stars are auspicious.

Dangerous Palaces

All houses are affected by the 5 yellow star, which in 2002 has flown to the east. Unfortunately the east also has the main star 5, and the combination of two 5s can, and usually does, have a deadly effect. This applies to all houses during the year, irrespective of their orientation. The effect of the Five Yellow is felt most in months two and eleven (i.e. in March and December), when the monthly 5 also comes visiting the east palace. Anyone with a bedroom located in the east is certain to succumb to illness. Keep plenty of fresh flowers in the east to strengthen its intrinsic element *chi* of wood, since this has the power to control the Five Yellow.

The south, meanwhile, is also very afflicted this year. The annual 2 star enters the *Li* palace and creates an atmosphere that is extremely fiery and earthy in nature. While this is sometimes regarded as auspicious in terms of wealth creation if the natal chart stars are strong, nevertheless this configuration implies that this is at the expense of health and relationships. A level of unhappiness is indicated for residents of this sector. They will also succumb to stress and strains of working life in the process of climbing up the career ladder. Do be careful of overworking and getting sick.

Month-by-Month Analysis

☆ MONTH 1: February 4–March 6

Good fortune comes this month. The wealth cycle moves upward, although there are hostile challenges. Do not lend money to friends, or you might lose them. There is hard work in store but the results are worth it. Those residing in the south palace will have to endure the stress of disagreements and hostility at work, and this will definitely impede progress. Place an urn of *yin* (still) water here to help overcome this problem.

Residents in the southwest must be extra careful in their relationships. Loss, betrayal, and illness are indicated, so be careful.

The west encounters good career luck this month. Circumstances at work are favorable. However, do note that the monthly 1 star is in direct conflict with the annual 9, bringing much illness relating to water and the stomach caused by energy being too *yang*.

☆ MONTH 2: March 6–April 5

The southeast benefits from the double 6 stars, which cause the focus this month to be on family and authority issues in the office. There are hiccups at work but mentor luck is strong. Business and money luck are sluggish.

The northwest enjoys abundance and prosperity, with smooth sailing in business and social life! There will be lots of opportunities to start new ventures. If you can use a northwest door to enter the house this month, it will be exceedingly auspicious. This is how feng shui can enhance your luck. Just use the back door and the feng shui of the whole house becomes auspicious. The north suffers great setbacks this month. Embezzlement in your company causes problems. There could also be legal entanglements. The south suffers from extreme bad illness luck.

☆ MONTH 3: April 5–May 6

Luck is bad this month. The monthly 5 comes to the southeast, bringing business to a standstill. To overcome this poor feng shui, move to a more auspicious room. If you cannot move out of the southeast, then hang six-rod windchimes there. The north and southwest are also afflicted. The good luck spots in the house this month are the south and northwest. Residents in both sectors will enjoy good fortune in travel and money matters.

☆ MONTH 4: May 6–June 6

The monthly 4 star enters the southeast, bringing with it the luck of academic advancement, proficiency, elegance, and romantic flirtation. The 4 star exerts great influence when it enters its original palace – the southeast. Unfortunately, its power, when combined with the annual 6, is not helpful for women. This is made worse by the water star being the unfortunate 5.

The lucky sector this month is the northwest, where residents enjoy the luck of career and easy success. The northwest has tremendous good luck, especially pertaining to career, commerce, and business. Single people living in the southeast sector will have opportunities for serious romance. The sum of ten (monthly 4 with annual 6) is also auspicious and this combination can either be very good or harmful for the women of the family. Use windchimes to protect and enhance at the same time. The windchime strengthens the 6, while getting rid of bad vibes that can sometimes get associated with the 4 star (especially when there is water in or near the entrance palace).

☆ MONTH 5: June 6–July 7

The incoming monthly 3 in the southeast brings conflicts into the household. But this combination can also bring an unexpected windfall. Place a cluster of crystals in the southeast this month to activate this palace. Those in the northwest sector should stay away from romantic affairs. Note that here the monthly 5 star here afflicts the otherwise lucky star numbers, thereby causing some setbacks in business and money luck. Do not make hasty decisions concerning new investments or expansions. It's better to lie low this month.

The auspicious location this month is the south. Wealth and career luck are good here and there is promotion or increase in income.

The southwest enjoys slightly improved luck. Please note that while the month is good, the natal chart has a bad configuration of 5 and 3, so health as well as communication with people can be a problem.

☆ MONTH 6: July 7–August 8

This month sees some health setbacks. The unlucky 2 enters the southeast, bringing sickness *chi*. Usually a 6/2 combination brings unexpected good fortune but because this house has a 5 water star here it suggests problems instead. These can be rather severe, especially concerning money and cash flow. So watch out. If your door is in the east or south, the luck is considerably better. It is the southeast that is afflicted this month.

Career and business suffers. Make certain that you personally check everything and don't take chances. In both financial and love matters, exercise restraint and caution. Watch out for backstabbing and traitors from within.

Prospects for love will be in the northwest this month. The young and single will enjoy a wonderful time falling in love, but as romance luck is brought by the monthly 4 star, it is always good not to go overboard and overreact. Stay cool.

☆ MONTH 7: August 8–September 8

This month the 1 enters the southeast, and this combines beautifully with the annual 6 star, bestowing residents of the house with good fortune for the month. The luck cycle begins to move upward very quickly. This is the time to make advancements. There will be progress at work. There is financial gain and young members of the household benefit the most from the good fortune. Good luck also enters the southwest this month, where the auspicious 8 star brings improvements and some wealth luck. Use this good timing to make the improvements needed to succeed.

The 5 star afflicts the northeast, which could cause distractions to those attending school. Use a strong cluster of crystals to overcome this affliction.

☆ MONTH 8: September 8–October 8

In the eighth month we see the monthly star 9 entering the southeast palace. The presence of fire and metal in a *Sun* environment suggests a great deal of disharmony and imbalance being created. Metal and fire *chi* battle in a wood environment – so here the wood suffers from being exhausted and destroyed by two unfriendly elements. Luck therefore becomes unstable and uncertain.

☆ MONTH 9: October 8–November 7

The cycle of luck improves substantially in the ninth month, when the 8 combines with the 6 in a *Sun* palace i.e. the southeast – this auspicious combination of white stars 8 and 6 brings relationship and prosperity luck and hence popularity and wealth. They bring many double happiness (*hei see*) occasions including a birth, longevity celebrations, and weddings. The

SE/NW axis is also most auspicious this month since the 1 monthly star visits the northwest. This combines with the annual 8 star in the palace, thereby enhancing the luck of the household. A lucky axis always brings good fortune which does not need to be activated. Some residents may find "turn-around" miracles, or unexpected gains from work and business. Income is derived from various sources and there is smooth sailing in all ventures.This is an auspicious time to start a family as children born or conceived this month will have a bright future. The south enjoys "peach blossom" luck this month, caused by the entry of love stars. Do exercise restraint, however, since there is danger of excesses causing scandals. The north is badly afflicted. The 5 may cause life-threatening situations because it combines with the hostile 3. Keep a rein on your temper! Please do not attempt to remedy this sector, it is incurable. The only thing to do is to move out of your north room. Do not embark on a holiday this month if your room is in the north. If you try to "escape" you may have an accident on the road.

☆ MONTH 10: November 7–December 6

The lucky and unlucky sectors are the same as month one.

☆ MONTH 11: December 7–January 4, 2003

The lucky and unlucky sectors are the same as month two.

☆ MONTH 12: January 5–February 3, 2003

The lucky and unlucky sectors are the same as month three.

A Southwest 1 House or Building

Facing 202.5 to 217.5 degrees

The natal chart for a **Southwest 1** house in the year 2002 is shown on the left.

In the chart please note that the annual numbers in each grid are those in pink placed at the bottom right-hand corner.

The numbers in black represent the house natal chart. These numbers are also the period 7 numbers, and are referred to as the main numbers. The small numbers to the right of the main numbers are the water star numbers, while the small numbers on the left are the mountain star numbers.

General Outlook for the Year

Please note that the annual chart numbers are exactly the same as the period numbers in the year 2002. This is because the *Lo Shu* number for 2002 is 7, so the number 7 is in the center. The strengthening of the *Lo Shu* 7 is excellent for a building where the main star 7 combines with the good mountain and water stars in the center, as is the case for those of you living in a house or apartment building that is oriented to face the southwest 1 direction.

The annual 4 lucky star visits the southwest palace in 2002, bringing exceptional good fortune for those engaged in the communication business. Writers and advertising people will enjoy great good fortune, especially if they are west-group people. This auspicious indication is further strengthened by the equally auspicious northeast, which makes the axis (SW/NE) extremely fortunate. Those living in southwest 2/3 houses also enjoy this same lucky situation. Note that the northeast has a wonderful concentration of the 1 white stars.

In this southwest 1 house all the good fortune palaces are located inside, at the back of the house. However, the entrance sector is also very auspicious because it enjoys the double 7 in its natal chart and the double 4 in its 2002 chart. The combination is really very sound and stable. Those with this house orientation have just come out from a bad and afflicted year, since in 2001 the southwest suffered from the presence of the Five Yellow. The turnaround of luck will therefore appear very dramatic indeed.

Wealth Luck

The wealth sector in the house is in the north, where the water star 8 is located. Here the combination with the mountain star is also very lucky, and the combination with the annual star 3 offers us a powerful *ho tu* combination. This benefits the house in terms of overall wealth luck, especially if this palace has been properly activated with a correct water feature (i.e. with *yang* (moving) water). However, this *chi* is too strong for children under the age of 12 so it is advisable to move young children to another sector.

Generally the wealth luck of this house will be good throughout this year of the water horse, mainly because the annual numbers for the house axis i.e. SW/NE are very favorable. This means that the front and back of the house enjoy good wealth stars. There is happiness for all those involved in the entertainment or media businesses, and in the marketing and advertising industries. Career professionals and consulting firms will enjoy excellent work luck. This comes about because the auspicious 1 star has flown into the northeast sector, which is already enjoying good luck brought by the 1 water star.

The year sees abundant opportunities and plenty of positive patronage from powerful and influential people. This is because the northwest enjoys the magical 8 star. Meanwhile, note that while money luck is strong, so too are the spending habits of residents. This year sees extravagance taken to new heights. The explanation, according to the ancient classics, is that the 7 water star in front (southwest) and the 1 water star at the back (northeast) lead to "water leaking out." So those of you who tend to overspend and live beyond your means can blame it all on the feng shui of your house!

Health Luck

The illness stars 2 and 5 are in the south and east respectively, thereby afflicting these two sectors. In the south there is also the 5/9 combination of mountain/water in the natal chart. Anyone residing in this palace will run the risk of falling quite seriously ill. The best remedy for this sector is to place metal windchimes to exhaust the much-strengthened afflicted earth energy.

It is the same in the east, where the risk to health is even more pronounced as it comes in the form of the annual Five Yellow. Since the *Lo Shu* number is also 5, the illness and loss star is very much strengthened. I certainly recommend that anyone staying here who may be suffering from some illness should move to a more vibrant and healthy sector. Once again windchimes will help to alleviate the situation.

Relationship Luck

Relationship and romance luck gets a huge boost this year because the annual 4 enters the entrance palace of the southwest. There are so many opportunities for happiness for those seeking to find love and romance. If you activate the southwest this year with all the love symbols, the effect will manifest itself very fast indeed. The good news is that there is nothing to indicate obstacles and problems along the way. Make sure, however, that there is no water placed in the vicinity of the southwest since this tends to bring out the darker side of the 4 star in terms of sexual escapades. This could result in malicious sexual rendezvous, that lead to heartache and disappointments. The good news once again for those keen on romance luck is that the numbers in the center of the house are very auspicious for romance.

Family and marital relationships, as well as interactions between your loved ones, will ripen into happiness this year. There will be few arguments. There is good fortune in romance luck for the young men and young women of the home who are looking for love, and marriage is possible. But take note ... romance does not necessarily mean that love will last forever. It is, however, a good year for marriage and engagements.

Prosperous Palaces

The southwest sector of the home enjoys excellent good fortune this year. For those engaged in finance and marketing, this sector brings great good fortune in the year of the water horse. This is especially pronounced because the double 7 represents gold and since the annual star in this palace is 4, there is an abundance of good luck. This is especially true for those in the communication business – TV and radio personalities living in this house will prosper.

The northeast palace of the home is also particularly lucky for career and academic pursuits. Those just embarking on careers and those studying or taking exams this year should use this part of the home simply because the star numbers are exceedingly favorable. The north room is also a favorable place for those who want to harness wealth luck. If your bedroom is here you will benefit from the water star 8, which brings money and success. The auspicious 8 annual star visits the northwest and this means that money luck is also strong here. More wealth can be generated through careful investments and diligent work.

Dangerous Palaces

All houses are affected by the 5 yellow star, which in 2002 has flown to the east. Unfortunately the east also has the main star 5, and the combination of two 5s can, and usually does, have a deadly effect. This applies to all houses during the year, irrespective of their orientation. The effect of the Five Yellow is felt most in months two and eleven (i.e. in March and December), when the monthly 5 also comes visiting the east palace. Anyone with a bedroom located in the east is sure to succumb to illness. Keep fresh flowers in the east to strengthen its intrinsic element chi of wood, since this has the power to control the Five Yellow.

The other danger palaces of a southwest-facing house are the south and southeast, which are both terribly afflicted by the natal chart stars and the annual chart stars. If given a choice, do not reside in these parts of the home. If you have no choice, use metal *chi* to control the 5/9 combination of the natal chart. In the south, this will also tire out the illness star 2 brought by the year chart. Meanwhile, there are two other sectors also afflicted by the horrible 2/3 combination of quarrelsome stars. These are the west and the northwest palaces. Make certain you do not hang windchimes in these two sectors. Instead use *yin* (still) water to create calm here.

The north is afflicted by the yearly Three Killings, which usually bring gossip, slander, and minor accidents. If this sector gets lively, with doors, excessive noise, or lots of people moving about, it gets activated. Thus, you should not renovate this sector nor play loud music here during the year. It's better to keep this sector quiet.

Month-by-Month Analysis

☆ MONTH 1: February 4–March 6

This first month sees the unlucky 5 star flying into the southwest, bringing with it bad vibrations. So the year does not start out well for southwest 1-facing houses. In addition, the illness 2 star flies into the northeast sector, so the SW/NE axis is quite seriously weakened in this first month. If you hung windchimes in these two sectors to overcome last year's bad stars, keep these in place for another month. A windchime placed in each of these sectors will control the month 5 star. Do not worry too much about the afflictions this month because things get better next month in a rather spectacular way. Be patient.

In this first month you can take heart from the fact that the star number in the center of the house is 8. This means that those homes with a wide-open center will benefit tremendously, since the 8 star will activate the exceedingly auspicious combination of numbers found in the center of this house natal chart.

☆ MONTH 2: March 6–April 5

This month brings excellent professional and career luck, due mainly to the double 4 combination in the southwest and the double 1 combination in the northeast. This makes the axis strong and prosperous indeed. There are good investment opportunities and excellent recognition at work, which can lead to promotion. Investment luck in the financial area is also strong – buy stocks in the communication business. Writers will enjoy renewed recognition and there are stunningly large rewards in store for hard work. It is a good time to seek new opportunities and start new businesses. Enhance career luck in the southwest with crystal globes and bright lights. Energize the northeast with a water feature. Those in the northwest, meanwhile, will benefit hugely from the double 8. This benefits the men of the family, who will enjoy the luck of sudden windfall profits.

☆ MONTH 3: April 5–May 6

In the third month, residents become aware of a certain competitive hostility creeping in. The 3 star brings envy and jealousy, which must be controlled by fire energy. Keep the center well lit all through this month and you will keep the 3 star at bay. A red lampshade is ideal for this purpose, as a surfeit of *yang* energy is what you need.

The 5 star visits the southeast, bringing illness and loss to residents. The northwest, however, continues to benefit from good stars such as the monthly 7. In the north beware the combination of monthly 2 with annual 3 – this brings bad vibes to the sector. Keep an urn of *yin* (still) water to absorb all the tension of this palace.

☆ MONTH 4: May 6–June 6

The monthly 2 star enters the southwest, bringing with it misfortune to those working in financial institutions and banks. It also indicates emotional setbacks, some danger of nervous breakdown due to overwork, and depression caused by excessive mental activity.

Healthwise be careful of contracting high fever, which may prove dangerous. The 2 month star flying into a 4 annual star and meeting with a mountain 7 star causes this. This configuration indicates a state of high fever. While indications of spiritual activities good, avoid overindulging in these practices as there is danger of getting carried away.

Avoid traveling far away from home. The 2 star meeting with the 7 mountain star can result in car accidents (2 = mishaps, 7 = metal vehicle). So be careful when driving this month. Wearing red should reduce the possibility of accidents.

The south palace is also afflicted. Here the monthly 9 visits the annual 2, thereby causing illness star 2 to get activated. Those occupying the northeast, however, will enjoy promotion at work while those in the southeast will enjoy new romantic involvements.

☆ MONTH 5: June 6–July 7

Money luck returns with a vengeance this month, and I can say that this is probably the best month of the year. There is danger of romantic involvement that could lead to problems, so be careful – don't get involved in romantic dalliances that will bring heartaches later. However, in terms of opportunities for making additional income, this is a most excellent month indeed.

Once again the axis has auspicious stars – the 1 star visiting the southwest and the 7 star visiting the northeast. Indeed in this month the SW/Center/NE, which forms the axis of a southwest house, has a terrific combination of numbers i.e. the stunning combination of 1, 4, and 7. In advanced Flying Star analysis this is known as a string combination and it is most auspicious indeed, especially since the natal chart numbers are also the same numbers! Those of you staying in this house should go all out this month as it is a most outstanding month indeed. You can invest with confidence and courage.

☆ MONTH 6: July 7–August 8

The good fortune continues and it could well be just as spectacular as last month. The southwest entrance palace has the 4/9 combination, and with the entry of the 9 star this once again becomes the very powerful *ho tu* combination. This combination brings exceedingly good luck for new ventures and start-up situations. At the back, in the northeast, we have the *ho tu* combination of 1/6, which brings awesome financial luck and commercial skills. Take advantage of this combination, and also energize it with metal objects – bells, coins, metal art, and windchimes. The 1/6 combination also benefits the second generation of the household.

☆ MONTH 7: August 8–September 8

Good fortune continues into the seventh month and this time it is brought by the 8 monthly star flying into the southwest palace. This month, however, the luck is considerably weakened by the star 2 in the center and the star 5 in the northeast. This means that the axis has become unstable, so it is a good idea to go slow and be extra careful. In the northwest, the hostile 3 has flown in to cause troublesome gossip for the patriarch, and in the east the 9 has flown in to strengthen the horrible 5. The indication this month, therefore, is for residents to tread warily. The lucky sectors this month (in addition to the southwest) are the south and southeast. The southeast enjoys the lucky 1/6 combination.

✰ MONTH 8: September 8–October 8

This month sees a repeat of the great good fortune of the fifth month, as once again we see the auspicious string numbers 1, 4, and 7 coming back. This time it is the 7 monthly star that flies to the southwest, combining with the annual star 4 there to make the *ho tu* combination. In the center grid the 1 star has flown in to join the 7 *Lo Shu* number, while in the northeast we see the 4 star flying in to complement the 1 star. All these combinations in these situations in a southwest 1 house are very auspicious indeed. There is the promise of making windfall gains from unexpected sources. There will lucky breaks and sudden elevations in income. Those engaged in the writing and literary fields will get a huge boost in their recognition luck. Everything will be quite spectacular.

Only the south is strongly afflicted because the 5 has flown there to combine horribly with the 2 star. So avoid the south and do not activate it in any way. Do, however, energize the SW/NE sectors with lots of crystal and earth energy. In the southwest, place a crystal globe to create even more wealth luck.

✰ MONTH 9: October 8–November 7

This month is something of an anticlimax after the activity of the previous month. The 6 flying into the southwest continues to bring good luck to the household. There is good financial luck and plenty of money-making opportunities. Residents will spend this month catching their breath, as the news coming in will be rather spectacular. Residents will get rich and even become famous. Those residing in the east palace of the house could get involved in an accident, so either move out of there or hang metal remedies in the sector to control the combination of 7 with 5 – this is a combination that spells misfortunes on the road.

The west will have problems relating to loss of money and the health of residents. What is indicated is that there could be hospitalization and surgery to do with the heart or the stomach area. Residents of the west sector would benefit from moving out of their room to try and escape this affliction.

☆ **MONTH 10: November 7–December 6**

The lucky and unlucky sectors are the same as month one.

☆ **MONTH 11: December 7–January 4, 2003**

The lucky and unlucky sectors are the same as month two.

☆ **MONTH 12: January 5–February 3, 2003**

The lucky and unlucky sectors are the same as month three.

A Southwest 2 or 3 House or Building

Facing 217.5 to 247.5 degrees

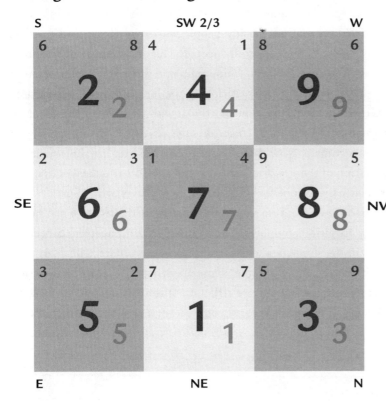

The natal chart for a **Southwest 2 or 3** house in the year 2002 is shown on the left.

In the chart please note that the annual numbers in each grid are those in pink placed at the bottom right-hand corner.

The numbers in black represent the house natal chart. These numbers are also the period 7 numbers, and are referred to as the main numbers. The small numbers to the right of the main numbers are the water star numbers, while the small numbers on the left are the mountain star numbers.

General Outlook for the Year

Please note that the annual chart numbers are exactly the same as the period numbers in the year 2002. This is because the *Lo Shu* number for 2002 is 7, so the number 7 is in the center. The strengthening of the *Lo Shu* 7 is excellent for this southwest-facing building, where the main star 7 combines with the good mountain and water stars in the center grid of its natal chart. This makes a southwest-facing house or apartment building very auspicious in this period of 7 and also in this year 2002.

Note the annual 4 lucky star visits the southwest palace in 2002, bringing exceptional good fortune for those engaged in the communication business. Writers and advertising people will enjoy great good fortune, especially if they are west-group people. This auspicious indication is further strengthened by the 4/1 mountain and water star combination in the southwest palace, thereby enhancing the luck indicated. In addition, there is the even more auspicious northeast with its double 7 combination of mountain and water stars. This makes the axis (SW/NE) very special and extremely fortunate. Note that the entire SW/NE axis has the wonderful concentration of the 1, 4, and 7 string numbers. This truly makes this year a particularly special one for southwest-facing houses.

In this southwest 2/3 house, all the palaces at the front of the house enjoy very auspicious numbers. The entrance sector is auspicious because it enjoys the 4/1 in its natal chart, and the double 4 in its 2002 chart. The combination is really very stable. Remember that the southwest direction and sectors suffered from severe affliction of the Five Yellow star in 2001, so this house orientation has just come out of a very badly afflicted year. The turnaround in luck this year will therefore appear to be very dramatic indeed.

Wealth Luck

The wealth sector in the house is in the south, where the water star 8 is located. Here the combination with the 6 mountain star is also very lucky, but the effect of the main star 2 and the annual star 2 creates a seriously dampening effect on the luck of the house. The south, being a fire corner, is also not a good place to install a water feature because of the direct clash between fire and water. The double 2 stars this year will bring illness to south sector residents.

Nevertheless, generally the wealth luck of this house is considered to be very good throughout this year of the water horse, mainly because the annual numbers for the house axis i.e. SW/NE are very favorable indeed.

This implies that both the front and back of the house enjoy good wealth stars along this axis. There is happiness for all those involved in the entertainment, communication, or media businesses, as well as in the marketing and advertising industries. Career professionals in the PR and publishing areas will enjoy excellent work luck. This is derived from the very auspicious 4/1 combination in the southwest sector. Here the water star is 1 and the mountain star is 4, indicating good professional luck and good love luck. Romance will be strong for this house as well.

In the center grid are the 1, 4, and 7 numbers, which is a string combination. This is a very lucky set of three numbers and it indicates good fortune for a long, long time. At the back, in the northeast sector, we see the most auspicious double 7 mountain and water stars, with the double 1 of the annual and *Lo Shu* numbers – all indicating a very propitious state of affairs.

The indications therefore suggest abundant opportunities and plenty of real money luck. Even though there are other sectors quite severe afflictions, nevertheless this powerful axis line is extremely beneficial.

Health Luck

Healthwise the afflicted sectors are the east and north. This is mainly because this year the Five Yellow is in the east, where it creates a double whammy by combining with the *Lo Shu* 5 star. So it best to avoid having a bedroom in the east. The north, meanwhile, is afflicted by the 5/9 combination and this is made worse by the annual and *Lo Shu* number 3. This concentration of tough numbers makes this an unhealthy sector.

Relationship Luck

Relationship and romance luck gets a very big boost this year, especially for all of you who are single and available. It could even be a year of marriage. This is because the annual 4 enters the entrance palace of the southwest. The center number is 4 and the mountain star is also 4 – this excess of the love number in flying stars means that there will many opportunities for happiness for those seeking love and romance.

If you activate the southwest this year with all the love symbols – the double happiness symbol, the mandarin ducks etc. – the effect will manifest itself very fast indeed. The good news is that there is nothing to indicate obstacles and problems along the way. Make sure, however, that there is no water placed in the vicinity of the southwest as this tends to bring out the darker side of the 4 star in terms of sexual escapades – there is the danger of malicious sexual rendezvous, that lead to heartache and disappointments. The good news once again for those keen on romance luck is that the numbers in the center of the house are very auspicious for romance.

Prosperous Palaces

The southwest sector of the home enjoys excellent good fortune this year. For those engaged in finance and marketing, this sector brings great good fortune in the year of the water horse, brought especially by the powerful 1 water star. This is just so beneficial for the house! The 4 in the southwest indicates that wealth luck smiles on anyone involved in the profession of writing.

The northeast is also particularly lucky for career and academic pursuits. Those just embarking on careers and those studying or taking exams this year should use this part of the home simply because the star numbers are exceedingly favorable. The northeast room is a favorable place for those who want to harness wealth luck. If your bedroom is here you will benefit from the double 7 water and mountain star, which brings money and success during this period of 7. Of course, we have to note that the period of 7 is coming to a close soon and this means that the energy of 7 is on the decline. It is a good idea therefore to activate the 7 with metal energy – so placing coins, bells, and metal art in this corner is an excellent idea.

Dangerous Palaces

All houses are affected by the Five Yellow star, which in 2002 has flown to the east. Unfortunately the east also has the main star 5, and the combination of two 5s can, and usually does, have a deadly effect. This applies to all houses during the year, irrespective of their orientation. The effect of the Fivr Yellow is felt most in months two and eleven (i.e. in March and December), when the monthly 5 also comes visiting the east palace. Anyone with a bedroom located in the east is certain to succumb to illness. Keep plenty of fresh flowers in the east to strengthen its intrinsic element *chi* of wood, since this has the power to control the Five Yellow.

It is vital to remember that you must not undertake any renovations in the east sector at all. Otherwise good fortune becomes misfortune. In fact, you should not even cut down trees in the east sector or everyone living in the house will get sick. Thus health is the main issue of concern in the east. The annual 5 star is very destructive when it meets with the main star 5. This gives lots of problems mentally and emotionally. It also weakens your health considerably.

The north is afflicted by the annual Three Killings. The Three Killings can bring gossip, slander, and minor accidents if activated. Thus, it is advisable not to do any renovations this year in this sector. The auspicious 6 star visits the southeast this year, but despite this auspicious happening the natal charts show a bad mountain and water star combination.

Month-by-Month Analysis

☆ MONTH 1: February 4–March 6

This first month sees the unlucky 5 star flying into the southwest, bringing bad vibrations to the sector. So the year does not start out well for southwest-facing houses. At the same time also, the 2 illness star flies into the northeast sector so the SW/NE axis is quite seriously weakened in this first month. If you hung windchimes in these two sectors to overcome last year's bad stars, keep these in place for another month. A windchime placed in each of these sectors will control the monthly 5. Do not worry too much about the afflictions this month because things get better in the coming months in a rather spectacular way. Be patient.

In this first month you can take heart from the fact that the star number in the center of the house is 8 so those homes with a wide open center will benefit tremendously since the 8 star will activate the exceedingly auspicious combination of numbers found in the center of this house natal chart.

☆ MONTH 2: March 6–April 5

This month brings excellent professional and career luck, due to the double 4 combination of period and annual stars in the southwest sector. The natal chart stars of 4/1 here also add to the luck-bringing 4, enhanced by the 1. Water feeds wood and this is reflected in this combination. There are good investment opportunities and excellent recognition at work, which can lead to promotion. Investment luck in the financial area is also strong – buy stocks in the communication business. Writers will enjoy renewed recognition and there are stunningly large rewards in store for hard work. It is a good time to seek new opportunities and start new businesses. Enhance career luck in the southwest with crystal globes and with bright lights.

Energize the northeast with a water feature. In the northeast, the double 7 combination is enhanced by the annual star 1, but afflicted by the monthly star 2. The SW/NE axis is very strong, bringing good fortune to the house. Those in the northwest benefit hugely from the double 8. This is better for the men of the family, who enjoy the luck of sudden windfall profits.

☆ MONTH 3: April 5–May 6

In the third month, residents experience a certain competitive hostility creeping in. The 3 star brings envy and jealousy, but this can be controlled by fire energy. Keep the center well lit all through this month and you will keep the 3 star at bay. A red lampshade is ideal for this purpose since a surfeit of *yang* energy is what you need.

The 5 star visits the southeast bringing illness and loss to residents, but the northwest continues to benefit from good stars. The 7 enters into the northwest.

In the north beware the combination of monthly 2 with annual 3 – this brings bad vibes to the sector. Keep an urn of *yin* (still) water to absorb all the tension of this palace.

☆ MONTH 4: May 6–June 6

The monthly 2 star enters the southwest, bringing with it misfortune to those working in financial institutions and banks. It also indicates too many emotional demands being made on residents, and there is some danger of problems associated with matters of the heart. Healthwise be careful of contracting sexually transmitted diseases, which may prove dangerous. The 2 month star flying into a 4 annual star and meeting with a mountain 4 star causes this excess of emotional and mental energy. This configuration indicates a state of tension and high pressure. While love is flattering and romance keeps you on a high, too much could also lead you into trouble. So stay cool.

The south palace has a very auspicious natal chart, for the 8 water star is found here. The monthly 9 visits the annual 2, causing the 6/8 stars to get activated and this is good for the house. Those occupying the northeast benefit from the month 8 star and will enjoy promotion at work, while those in the southeast will enjoy new romantic involvements.

☆ MONTH 5: June 6–July 7

Money luck returns with a vengeance this month, and I can say that this is probably the best month in the year. There is danger of romantic involvement that could lead to problems. So be careful – don't get involved in romantic dalliances that bring future heartaches.

However, in terms of opportunities for making additional income, this is a most excellent month indeed. Once again the SW/NE axis has auspicious stars, the 1 star visiting the southwest and the 7 star visiting the northeast.

When you examine the entire line of numbers in the SW/Center/NE line or axis, you will note that this month the axis of a southwest house has a terrific combination of numbers i.e. the stunning combination of 1, 4, and 7. In advanced Flying Star analysis this is known as a string combination and it is most auspicious indeed, especially since the natal chart numbers are also the same numbers! Those of you staying in this house should go all out this month, as it is a most outstanding month indeed. You can invest with confidence and courage. When you use feng shui this way you will be practicing the most practical aspects of traditional classical feng shui, and should not be surprised when things begin looking up for you almost immediately. Remember that this book has precalculated most of the difficult stuff already. All you need to do is read, remember, and use the solutions given.

☆ MONTH 6: July 7–August 8

The good fortune continues and it could well be just as spectacular as last month. The southwest entrance palace has the 4/9 combination, with the entry of the 9 star. This is an illustrious *ho tu* combination, which is very powerful. This combination brings exceedingly good luck for new ventures and start-up situations. At the back, in the northeast, we see another *ho tu* combination of 1 with the monthly 6, which brings awesome financial luck and commercial skills. Take advantage of this combination. Place lots of metal objects – bells, coins, metal art, and windchimes to energize this combination. It is a combination that also benefits the second generation of the household.

☆ MONTH 7: August 8–September 8

Good fortune continues into the seventh month and this time it is brought by the 8 monthly star flying into the southwest palace. This month, however, the luck is considerably weakened by the monthly stars 2 in the center and 5 in the northeast.

This means that the axis has become unstable, so it is a good idea to go slow and be extra careful. In the northwest the hostile 3 has flown in to cause troublesome gossip for the patriarch, and in the east the 9 has flown in to strengthen the horrible 5. The indication this month, therefore, is for residents to tread warily. The lucky sectors this month (in addition to the southwest) are the south and the southeast. The southeast enjoys the lucky 1/6 combination.

☆ MONTH 8: September 8–October 8

This month sees a repeat of the great good fortune of the fifth month where once again we see the auspicious string numbers 1, 4, and 7 coming back. This time it is the 7 monthly star that flies to the southwest, combining with the annual star 4 there to once again make the *ho tu* combination. In the center grid the 1 star has flown in to join the 7 *Lo Shu* number while in the northeast we see the 4 star flying in to complement the 1 star. All these combinations in these situations in a southwest 2 or 3 house are very auspicious indeed. There is the promise of making windfall gains from unexpected sources. There will be lucky breaks and sudden elevations in income. Those engaged in the writing and literary fields will get a huge boost in their recognition luck. Everything will be quite spectacular.

Only the south is strongly afflicted because the 5 has flown there to combine horribly with the 2 star. So avoid the south and do not activate it in any way. Do, however, energize the SW/NE sectors with lots of crystal and earth energy. In the southwest, place a crystal globe to create even more wealth luck.

☆ MONTH 9: October 8–November 7

This month is something of an anticlimax after the activity of the previous month. The 6 flying into the southwest continues to bring good luck to the household. There is good financial luck and plenty of moneymaking opportunities. Residents will spend this month catching their breath, as the news coming in will be rather spectacular. Residents will get rich and even become famous.

Those residing in the east palace of the house could get involved in an accident so either move out of there or hang metal remedies in the sector to control the combination of 7 with 5 – this is a combination that spells misfortunes on the road.

The west will have problems relating to loss of money and threat to the health of residents. What is indicated is that there could be hospitalization and surgery to do with the heart or the stomach area. Residents of the west sector would benefit from moving out of their room here to try and escape this affliction.

☆ MONTH 10: November 7–December 6

The lucky and unlucky sectors are the same as month one.

☆ MONTH 11: December 7–January 4, 2003

The lucky and unlucky sectors are the same as month two.

☆ MONTH 12: January 5–February 3, 2003

The lucky and unlucky sectors are the same as month three.

A Northeast 1 House or Building

Facing 22.5 to 37.5 degrees

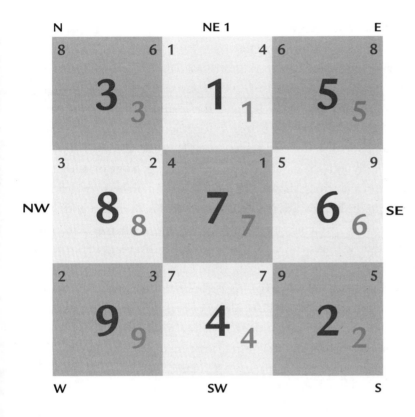

N   NE 1   E

8	6	1	4	6	8
	3 ₃		**1** ₁		**5** ₅

| 3 | 2 | 4 | 1 | 5 | 9 |
| **8** ₈ | | **7** ₇ | | **6** ₆ | |

NW   SE

| 2 | 3 | 7 | 7 | 9 | 5 |
| **9** ₉ | | **4** ₄ | | **2** ₂ | |

W   SW   S

The natal chart for a **Northeast 1** house in the year 2002 is shown on the left.

In the chart please note that the annual numbers in each grid are those in pink placed at the bottom right-hand corner.

The numbers in black represent the house natal chart. These numbers are also the period 7 numbers, and are referred to as the main numbers. The small numbers to the right of the main numbers are the water star numbers, while the small numbers on the left are the mountain star numbers.

General Outlook for the Year

Please note that the annual chart numbers are exactly the same as the period numbers in the year 2002. This is because the *Lo Shu* annual number for 2002 is 7, so the annual number 7 is also in the center grid. In a northeast 1-facing house the numbers in the center of the grid show an auspicious 4/1 combination which, when combined with the double 7, has an enhancing effect on the auspicious outlook for the house or building. If this house has an "open" center – which means there is no small room in the center of the home imprisoning the auspicious configuration of numbers – then the entire household will benefit from the good energy. This is because the center numbers are known as "string" numbers and these indicate long-lasting good fortune.

This year, the annual 1 enters the northeast palace. When the 1 star visits the *Ken* palace in the period of 7 it creates strong potential for lucky scenarios. The strength of the 1 annual star is enhanced by its interaction with the residing stars of the palace, so for a northeast 1 house, the basic interaction is with the 1 and 4 natal stars. Here the visiting 1 star is in harmony with both the mountain and water star – good news indeed!

Because of the strong showing of the 1, 4, and 7 numbers – which keep recurring in the NE/SW axis (and are also repeated in the center grid) – the northeast house will enjoy excellent good fortune in the year 2002. Even though this will generally not be an auspicious year, nevertheless, northeast-facing houses and buildings will benefit very much from the favorable strength of this axis. To enhance the facing palace i.e. the northeast itself, you should place plenty of healthy growing plants there. Do not place a water feature there since too much water could lead to problems associated with difficult romantic entanglements. In fact, when there is a water feature present in a 4/1 combination, the tendency is for there to be sexual scandals. And since the northwest palace has the contentious 3/2 combination in its natal chart, it is best not to encourage the creation of problems for the master of the household.

Wealth Luck

It is said in the classics that when the 4 water star is present in a palace it favors luck for those engaged in the communication and writing professions. And when there is also a 1 mountain star then it favors political luck. There is favorable publicity which leads to positive recognition for your work. If you wish to activate it for wealth, use slow-moving water but not too much since this runs the risk of the patriarch developing a roving eye. In any case, the numbers favor women more than men.

In this house the water star 8 is located in the east and a strong mountain star supports this also. The combination of 6 and 8 is always a good omen. However, in 2002 the annual star 5 comes in to create problems for the sector. The solution is to place plenty of metal energy here, not only will this exhaust the Five Yellow but it will also enhance the water star here. Another good sector for wealth is the southwest, where the double 7 is strongly complemented by the annual 4 star. While this brings problems in the area of romance, the 7 brings good income luck. Place slow-moving water here but only a small quantity. Do not use a lot of water to activate.

Health Luck

The northeast palace is looking vibrant and healthy and there does not seem to be major health problems in this house. However, in the east palace, the annual 5 drains the mountain star 6 and the water star 8, so residents here should take it easy.

The illness 2 is located in the south and this is probably the most afflicted sector of the house. Here the mountain/water star combination is the disturbing 9/5, which brings bad luck all round. It not only brings severe health problems, especially pertaining to the eyes, but there is also speculative loss of money as well. There is also the danger of fire hazards here, so it is a good idea to place an urn of *yin* (still) water to cool down the inflammation caused by the excessive energy. Do not place sick people in this part of the house, as their illness will deteriorate. Instead, move them to a more a healthy sector (northeast or southwest). Note that the same 9/5 combination is also repeated in the southeast sector, although here the annual star is the lucky 6. Nevertheless, it is wise to be careful if there are residents who are very sick.

Relationship Luck

There do not appear to be any special relationship-enhancing stars in the natal chart, although the mountain stars that govern relationship luck in the NE/SW axis sectors are auspicious. This indicates there will not be any major problems. However, the northwest sector, which offers clues to the luck of the patriarch, has the contentious 3 as its mountain star and this suggests that he will not find it all smooth sailing. The 8 annual star, however, does help him along. In the meantime, there is also a 3 water star in the west and this suggests that there is some misunderstanding to do with money matters afflicting residents staying in this sector. In fact, both the northwest and west have the unlucky 3/2 combination in their natal charts. However, while the northwest has the annual 8, the west has the annual 9, which means that the west is more severely afflicted. So for relationship luck, it is the front three palaces, the center grid, and the southwest which seem auspicious; the other four palaces will experience difficulty in interpersonal matters.

Prosperous Palaces

In the year of the water horse, the lucky sectors of the house in terms of prosperity luck are the southwest, northeast, north, and center palaces. The east sector has excellent natal stars but is afflicted by the Five Yellow. The southwest enjoys money luck brought by its double 7 and double 4 combination this year. The northeast palace benefits from the double 1 annual and main stars, while the north has auspicious natal stars. The combination of mountain star 8 with the annual 3 is also a *ho tu* combination so even though the 3 is contentious, nevertheless the combination of numbers is auspicious. The combination of the annual 3 star with the water star 6 indicates a time of slow growth. There is some danger to young men in this sector.

Dangerous Palaces

All houses are affected by the 5 yellow star, which in 2002 has flown to the east. Unfortunately the east also has the main star 5, and the combination of two 5s can, and usually does, have a deadly effect. This applies to all houses during the year, irrespective of their orientation, so it can be said that this year the auspicious east sector of a northeast 1 house is afflicted. The effect of the Five Yellow is felt most in months two and eleven (i.e. in March and December), when the monthly 5 also comes visiting the east palace. Anyone with a bedroom located in the east is certain to succumb to illness. Keep plenty of fresh flowers in the east to strengthen its intrinsic element *chi* of wood, since this has the power to control the Five Yellow.

The dangerous sector of a northeast 1 house this year is where the annual 5 yellow star resides, which is east. Fortunately, the evil nature of the 5 star is not very powerful in a northeast 1 house, but this does not stop the 5 star from bringing mishaps. There is a danger of misfortunes that can cause broken bones and limbs this year.

For those in the south, there are many annoying illnesses and matters that bog you down. This causes insomnia, making sleep fretful and fitful. The reading is that this sector will experience fatal injury and illnesses. It is not a bad idea to take up meditation and increase your physical activities. These activities will allow you to forget your worries. You could also move out of this palace. At the very least you are advised to use a great deal of metal as the sound of metal in the south sector will weaken the annual 2, as well as the horrible stars of the natal chart.

The southeast of the house is also dangerous due to the 5/9 in the natal chart, although the annual number 6 is auspicious. The west palace has the aggravating effect of the quarrelsome stars, which are further made more noisy by the fiery presence of the 9 annual star. Stay ever careful and place some *yin* (still) water here to calm things down.

Month-by-Month Analysis

☆ MONTH 1: February 4–March 6

This first month sees the unlucky 2 star flying into the northeast, bringing sickly energy vibrations to the sector. So the year does not start out good for northeast-facing houses. At the same time the deadly 5 star flies into the southwest sector, so the SW/NE axis is quite seriously weakened in this first month. Keep the windchimes you hung here in these two sectors to overcome last year's bad stars in place for another month to control the month stars 2 and 5 in these two important sectors of the house. However, do not worry too much about the afflictions because things will get better in the coming months. Be patient.

In this first month you can take heart from the fact that the star number in the center of the house is 8, so those homes with a wide-open center will benefit tremendously since this annual 8 star will activate the auspicious combination of numbers found in the center of this house natal chart.

☆ MONTH 2: March 6–April 5

This month brings excellent professional and career luck, due to the double 1 combination of period and annual stars in the northeast sector. The natal chart stars of 1/4 here also add to the luck-bringing water star 4, enhanced by the 1. The elements water and wood are most harmonious; there will be good investment opportunities and excellent prospects for promotion at work. Investment luck in the financial area is also strong – buy stocks in the communication and publishing industries. Writers will enjoy renewed recognition and there will be some good news coming. It is a good time to seek new opportunities and start new businesses. Enhance career luck in the northeast with crystal globes and bright lights.

Energize the southwest with a "mountain" feature. A painting of mountains or placement of crystals will be excellent. Here the double 7 combination is auspicious. However, the double 4 brings extreme bad luck from the opposite sex. Men should be careful not to get conned by conniving women with bad intentions, while women should beware of sweet talking Romeos! I would say that it is the women who are in greater danger than the men this month. This is because the northwest benefits hugely from the double 8, while the southwest has the double 4. This means that the men in the family enjoy smooth good fortune while the women also have good fortune but could get conned!

☆ MONTH 3: April 5–May 6

In the third month the fiery 9 enters the northeast, bringing career and money luck but also the potential for conflict. The presence of the 3 star in the southwest introduces the element of competitive hostility. The 3 star in the southwest brings envy and jealousy and, in fact, in severe cases this combination of the monthly 3 coming in to meet the annual 4 could well lead to some heartache. To overcome this, women in the household are advised to place strong fire energy here in the southwest. Also, keep the center of the house well lit all through this month and you will keep the 3 star in the southwest under control. A red lampshade is ideal for this purpose since a surfeit of *yang* energy is what you need.

The 5 star visits the southeast, bringing illness and loss to residents but the northwest continues to benefit from good stars with the entrance of the monthly 7.

In the north beware the combination of monthly 2 with annual 3 – this brings bad vibes to the sector. Keep an urn of *yin* (still) water to absorb all the tension of this palace.

☆ MONTH 4: May 6–June 6

The auspicious monthly 8 star enters the northeast, bringing with it excellent wealth luck. The presence of this number in the northeast is always auspicious because this is the "home" of the number 8, so this is the most auspicious month for this house during the year of the water horse. There could be some problems with partners and between siblings but these are small problems and can be ironed out without difficulty.

Healthwise be careful of contracting sexually transmitted diseases, which may prove dangerous. In the southwest, the 2 month star flying into a 4 annual star and meeting with a mountain 7 star causes an excess of emotional and mental problems. This configuration indicates love problems and some danger to the children. Take note that one-night stands might be flattering and seem romantic but the numbers in the southwest of your house are indicating that "love" or rather lust will only lead to trouble and heartaches. So stay cool. And stay aloof!

☆ MONTH 5: June 6–July 7

Money luck returns this month with the monthly 7 star flying into the northeast palace. In terms of money-making opportunities this is a very good month indeed. Once again this is caused by a very strong axis of auspicious stars. Just consider – the 7 star is visiting the northeast and the 1 star is visiting the southwest. So when you examine the entire line of numbers in the SW/Center/NE line or axis, you will note that this month the axis of a northeast house has a terrific combination of numbers i.e. the stunning combination of 1, 4, and 7. In advanced Flying Star analysis this is known as a powerful "string" combination, which is most auspicious indeed, especially since the natal chart numbers are also the same numbers!

Those of you staying in this house can go all out this month, as it is a very lucky month indeed. You can invest with confidence and courage. When you use feng shui this way you are practicing the most practical aspects of traditional classical feng shui and therefore shouldn't be surprised when things start looking up for you almost immediately.

If the center of your home is open and has lots of free space, it will be even more auspicious since the center numbers are very promising indeed. If the center is occupied by a store room or toilet, however, the good luck stays all locked up unless you keep the door opened. This is not possible, of course, if there is a toilet in the center!

☆ MONTH 6: July 7–August 8

The good fortune continues and it could well be just as spectacular as last month. In the northeast you have the month 6 coming in to meet the annual star 1, so the combination is the most auspicious *ho tu* combination. This suggests the entry of financial and career luck into the household. It also brings exceedingly good luck for new ventures and start-up situations.

You can enhance this further with the presence of metallic paintings or coins hung above the doorways into the room. At the back, in the southwest, we see another *ho tu* combination – the 4 annual with the 9 monthly, which also brings awesome start-up luck.

This combination indicates a most auspicious gestating period for whatever ventures you wish to launch. Place lots of metal objects – bells, coins, metal art, and windchimes to energize this combination. Take advantage of this combination. It also benefits the second generation of the household.

☆ MONTH 7: August 8–September 8

Good fortune takes a breather in the seventh month because the horrible star 5 has flown into the northeast palace. So although the 8 monthly star has flown into the southwest palace, the luck of the house has considerably weakened since the axis has become unstable. This is made worse by the star 2 flying into the center grid.

This means that it is a good idea to go slow and to be extra careful. In the northwest the hostile 3 has flown in to cause troublesome gossip for the patriarch, and in the east the 9 has flown in to strengthen the horrible 5 annual star. The indications this month, therefore, are for residents to tread warily. The lucky sectors this month (in addition to the southwest) are the south and southeast. The southeast enjoys the lucky 1/6 combination.

☆ MONTH 8: September 8–October 8

This month sees a repeat of the great good fortune enjoyed in the fifth month, as once again we see the auspicious string numbers 1, 4, and 7 coming back into play. This time the 4 star flying into the northeast complements the 1 star, bringing with it very good romance luck. In addition, the 7 monthly star flying into the southwest to combine with the annual star 4 once again makes the *ho tu* combination. In the center grid the 1 star has flown in to join the 7 *Lo Shu* number.

All these combinations in these situations in a northeast 1 house are very auspicious indeed. There is the promise of windfall gains from unexpected sources. There will lucky breaks and sudden elevations in income. Those engaged in the writing and literary fields will get a huge boost in their recognition luck. Everything is quite spectacular. The power of the 1, 4, 7 strings overrides almost all other afflictions in the three center palaces of the home. So luck is very strong this month.

Only the south is afflicted because the 5 has flown there to combine horribly with the 2 star. Avoid the south and do not activate it in any way. However, do energize the NE/SW sectors with lots of crystal and earth energy. In the northeast, place a crystal globe to create even more wealth luck.

☆ MONTH 9: October 8–November 7

This month is something of an anticlimax after the excitement of the previous month.

The 3 flying into the northeast attracts the green-eyed monster so there is some gossip and misunderstandings. However, the 6 flying into the southwest continues to bring good luck to the household. There is good financial luck and money-making opportunities. Residents will spend this month catching their breath, as the news coming in will be good all the way.

Those residing in the east palace of the house could get involved in an accident so either move out of there or hang metal remedies in the sector to control the combination of 7 with 5 – this is a combination that spells misfortunes on the road.

The west will have problems relating to loss of money and threat to the health of residents. What is indicated is that there could be hospitalization and surgery to do with the heart or the stomach area. Residents of the west sector would benefit from moving out of their room here to try and escape this affliction.

☆ **MONTH 10: November 7–December 6**

The lucky and unlucky sectors are the same as month one.

☆ **MONTH 11: December 7–January 4, 2003**

The lucky and unlucky sectors are the same as month two.

☆ **MONTH 12: January 5–February 3, 2003**

The lucky and unlucky sectors are the same as month three.

A Northeast 2 or 3 House or Building

Facing 37.5 to 67.5 degrees

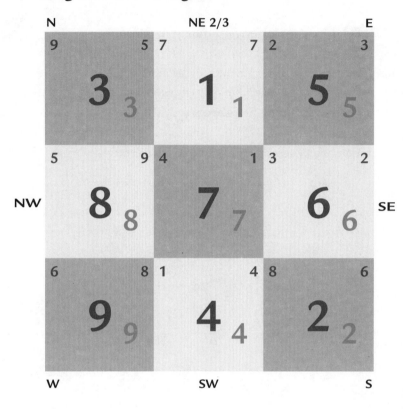

The natal chart for a **Northeast 2 or 3** house in the year 2002 is shown on the left.

In the chart please note that the annual numbers in each grid are those in pink placed at the bottom right-hand corner.

The numbers in black represent the house natal chart. These numbers are also the period 7 numbers, and are referred to as the main numbers. The small numbers to the right of the main numbers are the water star numbers, while the small numbers on the left are the mountain star numbers.

General Outlook for the Year

Please note that the annual chart numbers are exactly the same as the period numbers in the year 2002. This is because the *Lo Shu* number for 2002 is 7, so that the number 7 is in the center. The strengthening of the *Lo Shu* 7 is excellent for a building where the main star 7 combines with the good natal chart stars for mountain and water stars in the center, as is the case for those of you living in a house or apartment building that is oriented to face the northeast 2 or 3 direction.

The annual 1 lucky star visits the northeast palace in the year 2002, bringing exceptional good fortune for those engaged in the communication and publishing businesses. Writers and journalists as well as people in PR will enjoy good fortune, especially if they are westgroup people (see page 253). This auspicious indication is strengthened by the equally auspicious southwest, which makes the axis (NE/SW) extremely fortunate. Note that the northeast has a wonderful concentration of the 1 white stars this year.

In this northeast 2/3 house all the good fortune palaces are located at the back of the house. However, the entrance sector has the very auspicious double 7 in its natal chart, and it enjoys the double 1 in its 2002 chart. This combination is very stable, especially when we also consider the powerful string combination of numbers in its axis line formed by the northeast, the center, and the southwest palaces. This axis line has a combination of the string numbers 1, 4, and 7, which is especially lucky in this period of 7.

Wealth Luck

The wealth sector in the house is in the west, where the water star 8 is located. Here the combination with the mountain star is also very lucky. The 6/8 combination brings wealth, prosperity, popularity, and great richness. In fact, in flying star analysis, this is one of the most superior combinations. In the 2002 chart of this house the annual number is 9, which does not augur well for the sector since fire is not a good element in this palace. So the wealth palace is afflicted to some extent.

The northeast entrance palace has the double 7 and although the energy of the 7 star is waning, nevertheless it still brings prosperity luck. The 1 annual star here indicates extremely fortunate prosperity luck, but you will have to face very stiff competition in the market place.

Generally the wealth luck of this house will be good throughout this year of the water horse because the annual numbers for the house axis i.e. NE/SW are very favorable. This means that both the front and back of the house enjoy good wealth stars. There is happiness for all those involved in the entertainment and media businesses, and in the marketing and advertising industries. Career professionals and consulting firms will enjoy good work luck. This comes about because the auspicious 1 star has flown into the northeast sector, which is already enjoying good luck brought by the 7 water star. Residents thus experience abundant opportunities and patronage from influential people. This is because the northwest enjoys the magical 8 star. This attracts good fortune to the men of the household and the good annual star overrides the inauspicious natal star numbers.

Health Luck

The illness stars 2 and 5 are in the south and east respectively this year. This means that these two sectors are negatively afflicted this year. In the south there is the prosperous 8/6 combination of mountain/water in the natal chart. Thus the luck there is strongly positive, so the illness star will only bring hiccups and minor illnesses. To overcome the 2 star, use boulders tied with red thread as this will transform it into a more positive star. You can also use windchimes to exhaust it.

In the east the risk to health is more pronounced, and comes in the form of the annual Five Yellow. Since the *Lo Shu* number is also 5, the illness and loss star is very much strengthened. Also, here in the east, the natal chart numbers are inauspicious. The 2/3 combination indicates that there will be arguments and misunderstandings of the most serious kind. Illness and accidents are possible and you should use *yin* (still) water to try and soothe the *chi* here. Residents here might wish to consider moving out of the sector this year. I certainly recommend that those suffering from some illness should move to a more healthy sector.

Relationship Luck

Relationship and romance luck gets a big boost this year as the annual 4 enters the palace of the southwest, which usually governs relationships. The northeast entrance palace also has an auspicious mountain star 7. This means that there are opportunities for love, romance, and happiness for those who are looking.

If you activate the southwest this year with all the love symbols – the double happiness symbol, the mandarin ducks, and the mystic knot – the effect will manifest itself very quickly indeed. The good news is that there is nothing to indicate obstacles or problems along the way. Make sure, however, that there is no water placed in the vicinity of the southwest, since this could make the love and romance turn sour. Water tends to bring out the darker side of the 4 star, in that sexual rendezvous can turn malicious and lead to heartache. The good news for those keen on romance luck is that the numbers in the center of the house are auspicious for romance.

Family relationships and interactions between loved ones ripen into happiness this year. There is good fortune for the young men and young women of the home who want to get married, as their hopes materialize. But take note – romance does not necessarily mean that love will last forever.

Prosperous Palaces

The northeast palace of the home enjoys excellent good fortune this year. This is especially pronounced because the double 7 represents gold and since the annual star in this palace is 1, prosperity luck is assured. However, do take note that the environment will also prove to be very competitive. Place lots of gold ingots (the fake variety will do) or other forms of metal energy in the entrance palace and you sure to prevail over your competition.

Also use other wealth enhancers like a golden sailing ship or place six coins under the entrance mat to simulate hidden gold entering the home to help you. Whenever a palace has good auspicious stars, it is always a good idea to energize it with good fortune symbols. Just make sure that the element tends towards harmonizing with the intrinsic element of the sector. So note that the northeast is of the earth element and the trigram here signifies the mountain – when the numbers here are auspicious it suggests that the mountain is filled with gold. Since the number 7 is metal and is auspicious for this period, it means that gold has been mined at the entrance of the doorway. It is for this reason that northeast houses are said to be lucky this year.

The northeast palace of the home is also particularly lucky for career and academic pursuits. Those just embarking on careers and those studying or taking exams this year should use this part of the home because the trigram of this sector also favors study, and since the star numbers are favorable luck is said to be excellent.

Dangerous Palaces

All houses are affected by the 5 yellow star, which in 2002 has flown to the east. Unfortunately the east also has the main star 5, and the combination of two 5s can, and usually does, have a deadly effect. This applies to all houses during the year, irrespective of their orientation. The effect of the Five Yellow is felt most in months two and eleven (i.e. in March and December), when the monthly 5 also comes visiting the east palace. Anyone with a bedroom located in the east is sure to succumb to illness. Keep fresh flowers in the east to strengthen its intrinsic element *chi* of wood, since this has the power to control the Five Yellow. In a northeast 2/3 house the east also has the horrible 2/3 combination, so all the stars in the east of this house collectively spell disaster. I recommend that you move out of this room this year otherwise you will simply lose all your good luck. You could also have accidents and succumb to illness, which could prove fatal. You could also be engaged in litigation and other horrendous developments. Believe me, when bad luck comes to this kind of situation it can be very energy sapping. It's far better not to have to experience it. Move out of the east room if yours is a house with a northeast 2/3-facing direction. You should not delay doing this, and you should also not take this advice lightly. This is the reason you bought this book – because your karma is good and hence you are reading this warning in ample time to do something about it.

The other dangerous palaces of a northeast-facing house are the north and northwest, which are both badly affected by the natal chart stars. Here the combinations of the mountain and water stars are 5 and 9. In the case of the north the natal chart stars are made worse by the 3 annual number, so you should really place some red and gold cures here.

The north is also afflicted by the yearly Three Killings, which bring gossip, slander, and minor accidents. If this sector gets lively with doors, excessive noise, or plenty of people moving about, it gets activated. Thus, you should not renovate this sector nor play loud music here during the year. It's better to keep this sector quiet and place an urn with *yin* (still) water to soothe the evil stars in this sector. The northwest, in contrast, enjoys the auspicious annual star 8 so the natal star numbers are kept at bay this year. Control them with a six-rod metallic windchime and the northwest will enjoy good fortune this year.

Month-by-Month Analysis

☆ MONTH 1: February 4–March 6

This first month sees the unlucky 2 star flying into the northeast bringing bad illness and causing vibrations to the sector. So the year does not start out good for northeast 2/3-facing houses. In addition, the 5 yellow star flies into the southwest sector so the NE/SW axis is weakened this first month. Hang windchimes in both sectors. Those residing in the southwest are advised to take a vacation, while those in the entrance palace of the northeast (e.g. if their bedroom is placed here) could suffer some problems in their marriage. Or there could be a car accident. Pregnant women should get out of this room as there is also danger of miscarriage.

☆ MONTH 2: March 6–April 5

This month brings excellent professional and career luck, due to the double 1 combination of period and annual stars in the northeast sector. The double 7 natal chart stars are energized, thereby bringing luck to the sector and the household. The double 7 suggests that you will prevail over the competition and money luck is present in large amounts. Enhance career luck here with crystal globes and bright lights. The southwest is also auspicious with the double 4 star. You can activate the sector with a mountain feature. A painting of mountains or placement of crystals is excellent. Here the natal chart combination of 1/4 brings popularity and political luck. Hence there is both power and influence.

☆ MONTH 3: April 5–May 6

In the third month the fiery 9 enters the northeast, bringing career and money luck but also the potential for conflict. The presence of the monthly 3 star in the southwest introduces an element of competitive hostility to the fortunes of the household. The 3 star in the southwest brings envy and jealousy and, in severe cases, the combination of the monthly 3 coming in to meet the annual 4 could lead to heartache and disappointment. This applies both to work and personal relationships. There is betrayal and disillusionment.

To overcome this, residents of the household are advised to create fire energy in the southwest. It is also a good idea to keep the center of the house well lit all through this month. By doing this the 3 star in the southwest will be kept under control.

Meanwhile, the 5 star visits the southeast, bringing illness and loss to residents here. The southeast already has the unlucky 3/2 combination so this is a danger sector in this third month. This month the northwest benefits from the monthly 7 star, which unites well with the 8 annual star. In the north beware the combination of monthly 2 with annual 3 star numbers – this brings bad vibes to the sector. Keep an urn of *yin* (still) water to absorb all the tension of this palace.

☆ MONTH 4: May 6–June 6

The auspicious monthly 8 star enters the northeast, bringing with it excellent wealth luck. The presence of this number in the northeast is always auspicious because this is the "home" of the number 8, so this is a very auspicious month for this house. Since the northeast also has the double 7 natal stars as mountain and water stars, the month star enhances this palace considerably.

Healthwise there is need to be careful. This is because the NE/SW axis of the house is severely afflicted in the center with the 5 illness and loss star and in the southwest with the 2 month star. In the Southwest the 2 is flying into a 4 annual star and meeting with a mountain 1 star – which indicates danger to women who are pregnant, and also illness affecting the internal organs. It is also a combination which causes bad luck to hit the marriage, so that there is danger of infidelity on the part of the husband. Discord could also occur between in-laws and especially between the wife and the mother-in-law. Some calm water would soothe ruffled feathers, and there is also a need to practice patience. Do not succumb to anger or temper tantrums since this could lead to extremely negative consequences.

☆ MONTH 5: June 6–July 7

Money luck returns this month with the monthly 7 star flying into the northeast palace. In terms of money-making opportunities this is a very good month indeed since there will be three 7s in the entrance palace. Since this is the period of 7, this is a very good situation. There is also a strong axis of auspicious stars. Note the 7 star is visiting the northeast, while the 1 star is visiting the southwest. When you examine the entire line of numbers in the SW/Center/NE axis, you will realize that this month the axis of a northeast house has a terrific combination of numbers i.e. the stunning combination of 1, 4, and 7. In advanced Flying Star analysis this is known as a powerful string combination which is very lucky and brings very powerful feng shui luck indeed, especially since the natal chart numbers are also the same numbers!

Those of you staying in this house can go all out this month, as it is a very lucky month indeed. You can invest with confidence and courage. When you use feng shui in this way you will be practicing the most practical aspects of traditional classical feng shui. You should therefore not be surprised when you see things looking up for you almost immediately.

If the center of your home is open with lots of free space, it will be even more auspicious since the center numbers are very promising indeed. If the center is occupied by a storeroom or toilet, however, the good luck stays all locked up unless you keep the door open. This is not possible, of course, if there is a toilet in the center! I want to stress this since the combination of numbers is rather special and it would be a shame to have it spoiled by a toilet blocking the flow of luck in the center. If you do have another toilet use it and leave the door of this one open.

☆ MONTH 6: July 7–August 8

The good fortune continues and it can be just as special as last month. Just consider ... in the northeast you have the month 6 coming in to meet the annual star 1, giving the most auspicious *ho tu* combination. This suggests the entry of financial and career luck into the household. It also brings exceedingly good luck for new ventures and start-up situations.

You can enhance this further with the presence of metallic paintings or coins hung above the doorways into the room. At the back, in the southwest, we see another *ho tu* combination – the annual 4 and the monthly 9 – which also brings awesome start-up luck.

☆ MONTH 7: August 8–September 8

Good fortune takes a break in the seventh month when the horrible star 5 flies into the northeast palace. So although the 8 monthly star has moved into the southwest palace, the luck of the house has considerably weakened as the axis has become unstable. This is made worse by the star 2 flying into the center grid.

In this month, therefore, it is better to slow down and be extra careful. In the northwest, the hostile 3 has moved in to cause troublesome gossip for the patriarch, and in the east the 9 has flown in to strengthen the horrible 5 annual star. The indication this month is that residents should tread warily. The lucky sectors this month (in addition to the southwest) are the south and the southeast.

230

☆ MONTH 8: September 8–October 8

This month sees a repeat of the great good fortune enjoyed in the fifth month, as once again we see the auspicious string numbers 1, 4, and 7 coming back into play. This time it is the 4 star flying in to the northeast to complement the 1 star, bringing with it very good romance luck. Add to this the 7 monthly star flying into the southwest to combine with the annual star 4 there, and once again you have the auspicious *ho tu* combination. In the center grid the 1 star has flown in to join the 7 *Lo Shu* number.

All these combinations in these situations in a northeast 2/3 house are very lucky indications. There is the promise of windfall gains from unexpected sources. There will also be lucky breaks and sudden elevations in income. Those engaged in the writing and literary fields will get a big boost in their fortunes. Everything is pretty special this month since the strength of the 1, 4, 7 string overrides most afflictions in the three center palaces of the home. So good luck is strong this month.

Only the south is afflicted because the 5 has flown there to combine horribly with the 2 star. So avoid the south and do not activate it in any way. Do, however, energize the NE/SW sectors with lots of crystal and earth energy. In the northeast, place a crystal globe to create even more wealth luck.

☆ MONTH 9: October 8–November 7

This month is something of an anticlimax after the excitement of the previous month. The 3 flying into the northeast attracts the green-eyed monster and this causes some tension, gossip, and misunderstandings. However, with the 6 star flying into the southwest, good luck continues to favor the household. There is money and romance luck and residents will stay happy this month as developments are positive.

Those residing in the east palace of the house could get involved in an accident so either move out of there or hang metal remedies in the sector to control the combination of monthly 7 with the annual 5 – this is a combination that spells misfortunes on the road. It is also a dangerous time to stay here in the east. Move out!

☆ **MONTH 10: November 7–December 6**

The lucky and unlucky sectors are the same as month one.

☆ **MONTH 11: December 7–January 4, 2003**

The lucky and unlucky sectors are the same as month two.

☆ **MONTH 12: January 5–February 3, 2003**

The lucky and unlucky sectors are the same as month three.

A Northwest 1 House or Building

Facing 292.5 to 307.5 degrees

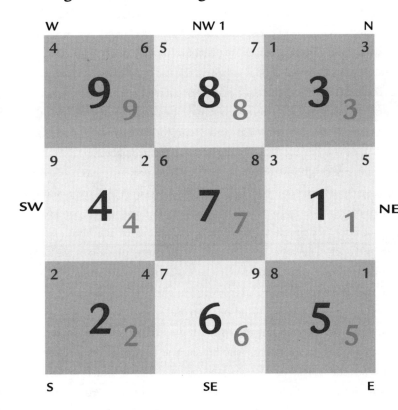

The natal chart for a **Northwest 1** house in the year 2002 is shown on the left.

In the chart please note that the annual numbers in each grid are those in pink placed at the bottom right-hand corner.

The numbers in black represent the house natal chart. These are also the period 7 numbers, and are referred to as the main numbers. The small numbers to the right of the main numbers are the water star numbers, while the small numbers on the left are the mountain star numbers.

General Outlook for the Year

Please note that the annual chart numbers are exactly the same as the period numbers in the year 2002. This is because the *Lo Shu* number for 2002 is 7, so the number 7 is in the center. The strengthening of the *Lo Shu* 7 in the center is an excellent enhancer for a northwest-facing house, which has the very auspicious 6/8 combination at its center grid. This means that the annual chart strengthens the positive aspects of the natal chart. This implies that 2002 is an excellent year for northwest-facing houses and buildings.

In the case of the northwest 1-facing house, the double 8 scenario complements the auspicious 7 water star at the entrance palace. This implies a situation of good prosperity luck. Whenever the 8 star comes into a place with the 7 star, the effect is to strengthen the prosperity effects of the 7 star during this period of 7. It brings the luck of success and winning, so that residents will find they can easily prevail over their competitors and adversaries. The outlook in terms of career, business, and investments is therefore very good for this year and I cannot overstress the excellent positioning of the double 8 star being at the entrance palace.

In the center of this house the natal chart stars are very auspicious – here we see the auspicious water star 8 and the equally auspicious mountain star 6, a combination that is hard to beat. The household enjoys wealth, prosperity, and popularity. This manifests strongly if the center of the home is kept spacious and open. The larger the floor area of the center portion of the home, the luckier the home will be. However, if there is a toilet in the center, the good stars are said to be seriously afflicted. If the kitchen is located here it is also not a good thing. The center should be open and spacious.

For those of you who might be wondering whether you should activate the water star 8 in the center of the house, the answer is yes – especially since the annual star 7 is also in the center. This would be the most important feature to create if what you want is the luck of prosperity. The best water features are those that flow in a slow manner. Fountains are good but flows are better. Aquariums are also a good way to activate water. I would like to point out, though, that water needs to move and to have life in it for it be *yang* – and this means either having fish or plants in the water. Fake plastic fish are quite useless as wealth energizers.

Wealth Luck

The wealth luck of this house will generally be good throughout this year of the water horse. There is happiness for those involved in the metal and food industries. Those with careers in the real estate business will also do well this year. However, it is those who are involved in metal, oil, and jewelry businesses that will benefit most from living in a northwest-facing house.

The most auspicious part of the house is in the center, where the 6/8 combination promises both wealth luck as well as harmony in all matters pertaining to relationship luck. This comes from the excellent mountain and water stars. There will be opportunities for making good investments, as well as for getting into upwardly mobile careers.

Another auspicious sector is the west palace, where the water star 6 creates good vibes. Here the annual star 9 brings money luck as it combines favorably with the water star, but there could also be a great deal of friction between the generations. Children do not appreciate the viewpoint of their parents. The 4/6 combination of the natal chart also brings money luck, but it is negative for women. Pregnant women should stay out of this sector.

Health Luck

The 5 annual star in the east brings afflictions to an otherwise auspicious sector. Here the natal chart combination of 8/1 suggests that there is excellent prosperity luck and career advancements, but these number combinations also suggest sibling rivalry. Generally, however, luck is good. The 5, however, brings severe afflictions to this sector in 2002 and it is a good idea to control the Five Yellow with six-rod windchimes. Another remedy is to place plenty of plants here.

The sickness star 2 is in the south. This sector is very seriously afflicted by the configuration of 2s here. Indeed, there are three 2s here in this south palace – a dangerous indication indeed. In the months two and eleven (i.e. March and December) the threat of fatal illness becomes more grave as the monthly star 2 flies in. This suggests that the south sector's illness affliction is extremely serious. I strongly advise that if this is the natal chart of your house, no one should stay in the room that is located in the south. Do take this piece of advice seriously since the potential for contracting a fatal disease – which may have to do with the heart, the womb, or the stomach – is very real. Place lots of metal energy in this sector and keep any room here locked up for the year. Placing an urn of *yin*, or quiet, water in this sector should also disarm the mountain star 2. Change the water every week so it does not get too excessively *yin*.

Relationship Luck

Relationship luck in a northwest house is certainly not strong. This is because the mountain star in the entrance palace of the northwest is the deadly 5 star. This is considered most unfortunate, especially since the water star is 7. This is a combination that implies constant arguments – and residents of this house could also be susceptible to mouth-related diseases. The way to overcome the bad relationship luck is to energize the 7 water star while controlling the 5 mountain star.

Do this by having a water feature here to create a situation of "mountain falling into the water." To strengthen this cure, hang a six-rod windchime on the wall near the entrance – both inside and outside the house. This stimulates and energizes the 7 star while keeping the 5 star under control.

There is another reason why the relationship luck of this house is said to be somewhat lacking. This is because of the mountain and water star combination in the southwest. Here the water star 2 and the mountain star 9 create a situation of extreme bad luck. Things cannot succeed due to the personality problems that will manifest themselves in every situation. Children should not reside in this palace. One way to reduce the impact of this negativity is to place fresh flowers and healthy green plants in this sector. This does not make relationship luck good but it will reduce the severity of animosity and hostility.

Prosperous Palaces

The center and the east are the two major sectors of wealth in this house, based on the natal chart, but the 5 star heavily afflicts the east this year. Otherwise the east sector is actually good for both wealth and power! This house will be excellent for those who are considered to be west-group people under the Eight Mansions formula of feng shui, (see page 253) and especially for those whose self element under this formula is earth. This enables them to overcome the 5 star, allowing the full force of the natal chart numbers to come into play. Generally, however, treat the east with caution and tread warily.

The northwest sector of this home has good fortune this year. The double 8 will make certain of that, so that those involved in commerce, retail sales, and marketing will benefit from customer loyalty and increasing popularity. These developments will translate into profit increases. The west also enjoys some money luck but creativity tends to dry up.

Dangerous Palaces

All houses are affected by the 5 yellow star, which in 2002 has flown to the east. Unfortunately, the east also has the main star 5, and the combination of two 5s can, and usually does, have a deadly effect. This applies to all houses during the year, irrespective of their orientation. The effect of the Five Yellow is felt most in months two and eleven (i.e. in March and December), when the monthly 5 also comes visiting the east palace. Anyone with a bedroom located in the east will surely succumb to illness this year. In this northwest house, however, the danger from the Five Yellow has been considerably reduced by the presence of the auspicious natal chart numbers. Both mountain and water stars are very auspicious in the east.

The north sector is the area of bad news because the Three Killings reside here this year. Make certain that you do not undertake renovations in the north. If you have to renovate, please choose a good date and make sure you do not begin or end your renovation work in this sector.

Money is the main issue of concern in the north. The annual 3 is very destructive, especially when it meets with the mountain 3. This creates a great deal of interpersonal problems. So my advice is to move out of the north room and close all windows and doors facing north.

Month-by-Month Analysis

☆ MONTH 1: February 4–March 6

The year starts with a bang for this house with the arrival of the fiery and dogmatic monthly 9 star in the northwest. This is a fortunate month which is excellent for money and for celebrations. There is promotion and additional power thrust on your shoulders. You could also be head-hunted with tempting offers. Whatever your decisions on the career front you are on a roll ... so do whatever makes you happy. You can commence a new business and become an entrepreneur. You will meet good partners for whatever venture you wish to be in.

In this month, though, the 9 combines with the 8 annual star to create severe problems between father and son. There will be problems with the children of the household and misunderstandings can turn nasty. The southeast is good for money and excellent for starting a family. This is a good room to use if trying for a child.

☆ MONTH 2: March 6–April 5

The second month brings wonderful good fortune to the home, and this manifests itself in elevation for the patriarch of the household. The double 8 star flies into the northwest palace, so that there are altogether three 8 stars here! This, along with the water star 7, makes a powerful combination indeed. Wealth gets created easily and residents benefit. The only danger is that there could be over-indulgence and during this lucky period residents should remember the advice of the *I Ching* – to behave with equanimity and generosity otherwise good fortune can easily transform into misfortune.

The other lucky sectors are the center of the house, where the double 7 also brings favorable developments, and the southeast, where the double 6 exerts its heavenly magic. The house is a happy house – good stars visit the central axis. Note how the 6, 7, and 8 in the center line are diverting beautiful *chi* into the household. Residents can take advantage of this by energizing these happy central palaces.

☆ MONTH 3: April 5–May 6

The monthly 7 star meets the annual 8 star in the northwest, bringing what is known as a "winning hand." The 7/8 combination brings victory and success over adversaries and competitors. The patriarch benefits the most this month.

All other sectors in the house are afflicted in some way or other. The southeast is visited by the very unlucky 5. The hostile 3 visits the southwest, thereby bringing quarrelsome luck to the women of the family. In the north, the illness star 2 brings a terrible influence to the annual 3 number here – all in all a good time to go on vacation! For the month itself it is a good idea to stay cool and not ruffle things too much. This is not a month to be too adventurous.

☆ MONTH 4: May 6–June 6

Wealth luck is good this month. The northwest enjoys the auspicious monthly 6 star as it enters the palace to combine with the annual 8. Luck is therefore high and prospects are excellent. This is one of the best combinations of numbers. There could be some tension in relationships between siblings and between husband and wife but this arises from trivialities and is nothing serious to worry about. At work there are some problems related to annoying politicking by small-minded troublemakers – the Chinese refer to such people as *siew-yan*, meaning "small person." Ignore these minor annoyances because the big picture is looking good.

The southeast is another fortunate palace. Here the 4 romantic star brings romance luck to a sector that is enjoying the prosperity luck of the annual 6. There could be an unexpected windfall for the residents here. However, because the southeast has the combination of 7/9 in its natal chart, and because this is a wood sector with so many metal stars, it is a good idea for nursing and expectant mothers to be extra careful should their bedroom be located here.

☆ MONTH 5: June 6–July 7

This month is most unpleasant. There is a lot of bickering, gossiping, and badmouthing. Residents will also have more than the usual number of stomach problems. Expectant mothers are advised to take extra care. Do not move heavy objects and most certainly do not sleep in the northwest. This is because the 5 star has flown into the northwest. Residents of this house should refrain from starting new ventures or getting married this month. Nothing started this month can last. Both money and relationship luck are headed for distress. Since relationship luck is also weak, avoid confrontation and do not start a new relationship this month.

The other unlucky palace is the east sector, which plays host to the illness star 2. Residents will easily succumb to health problems and lots of headaches. Those staying here could also be involved in accidents and hurt their heads.

☆ MONTH 6: July 7–August 8

The month brings favorable news for those engaged in the communications business. Students will also enjoy good luck in their studies and exams. The 4 star here in the northwest brings that kind of energy to the house. At the same time, the 4 also brings romance and lots of possibilities for happiness. It is therefore a favorable month. However, avoid sleeping in the west palace because the 5 has flown here. The annual 9 star causes the effect of this unfortunate star number to become exaggerated.

☆ MONTH 7: August 8–September 8

This is a month when advancement and progress come at some cost. There is hostile competition and a great deal of frayed tempers. Relationships will not be harmonious because of the 3 star entering the northwest and causing the auspicious annual 8 star to become afflicted. It is a good idea to move children to another room, and adults should keep control of their anger.

The southeast is lucky this month as the annual 6 star is enhanced by the entry of the 1 star. This combination brings success, prosperity, and happiness. At the same time it also belongs to the water element, and is excellent for the southeast sector, which is wood. There will thus be opportunities for success in business. The southwest, meanwhile, also enjoys good fortune and here the luck refers to both money and relationships.

This month the east has become rather dangerous so it is a good idea to stay away from this sector. The monthly 9 enters the east palace where the annual 5 star is located, and this suggests that the sector has become too inflamed by the fiery 9 star.

☆ MONTH 8: September 8–October 8

The entrance palace – the northwest – is harmed by the illness star 2. There is real danger of residents falling sick and although there continues to be good money luck, nevertheless you should hang a six-rod windchime here to control the 2 star number.

The south sector, meanwhile, has the dreaded 2/5 combination of annual and monthly stars so there is misfortune and extreme bad luck. Illness contracted here this month could be dangerous and could well prove to be fatal. Move to another room immediately and place metal energy here to keep the bad luck minimal and under control.

☆ MONTH 9: October 8–November 7

In the ninth month, the monthly stars of the house have turned friendly. Great good fortune visits the residents as the 1 star flies into the northwest and the 8 star flies into the southeast. This means both the front and back of the house benefits from extremely strong energy and although the center month 9 is not great, nevertheless the line stays auspicious because of the main star 7.

The sectors to avoid this month are the north, which is visited by the 5 star; and the west, which is visited by the 2 star. Both sectors bring bad luck to the residents. In the north there is also bad business luck that can be improved with the presence of water. The west numbers indicate that residents simply cannot find success this month. Children will be negatively affected in this sector this month.

☆ MONTH 10: November 7–December 6

The lucky and unlucky sectors are the same as month one.

☆ MONTH 11: December 7–January 4, 2003

The lucky and unlucky sectors are the same as month two.

☆ MONTH 12: January 5–February 3, 2003

The lucky and unlucky sectors are the same as month three.

A Northwest 2 or 3 House or Building

Facing 307.5 to 337.5 degrees

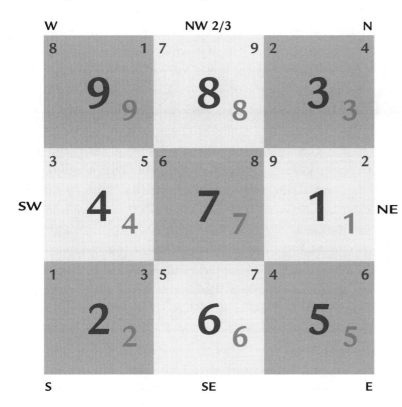

The natal chart for a **Northwest 2 or 3** house in the year 2002 is shown on the left.

In the chart please note that the annual numbers in each grid are those in pink placed at the bottom right-hand corner.

The numbers in black represent the house natal chart. These are also the period 7 numbers, and are referred to as the main numbers. The small numbers to the right of the main numbers are the water star numbers, while the small numbers on the left are the mountain star numbers.

General Outlook for the Year

Please note that the annual chart numbers are exactly the same as the period numbers in the year 2002. This is because the *Lo Shu* number for 2002 is 7, so the number 7 is in the center. The strengthening of the *Lo Shu* 7 in the center is an excellent enhancer for a northwest-facing house, which has the very auspicious 6/8 combination at its center grid. This means that the

annual chart strengthens the positive aspects of the natal chart. This implies that 2002 is an excellent year for northwest-facing houses and buildings.

In the case of the northwest 2/3 house, the double 8 scenario in the entrance palace of the house is excellent. However, unlike a northwest 1 house, the natal chart numbers here of 7 and 9, with the water star being 9, does not bring good indications. To start with, the combination suggests difficulties caused by weakness and lack of will power. The numbers of the natal chart are in conflict, so they destroy the luck of the sector.

Fortunately, the double 8, which is earth, brings strong energy to the northwest, which is metal. This implies a situation of good prosperity luck. Whenever the 8 star comes into a metallic palace, it brings wealth and gold to the sector. It brings success to residents, who will find it relatively easy to make things work. So the prospects for career and business are good this year. Place a cluster of crystals to further strengthen the good vibes in this corner of the northwest.

In the center of this house the natal chart stars are very auspicious – here we see the auspicious water star 8 and the equally auspicious mountain star 6, a combination that is hard to beat. Wealth, prosperity, and popularity are enjoyed by the household. These manifest themselves strongly if the center of the home is kept spacious and open. The larger the floor area of the center portion of the home the luckier the home will be. If there is a toilet in the center, however, the good stars are said to be seriously afflicted. If the kitchen is located here it is also not a good thing. The center should be open and spacious.

For those of you who might be wondering whether you should activate the water star 8 in the center of the house, the answer is yes – especially as the annual star 7 is also in the center. This would be the most suitable feature to create if you want prosperity luck. The best water features are those that flow in a slow manner. Fountains are good but flows are better. Aquariums are also a good way to activate water. I would like to point out, however, that water should move and have life in it for it be *yang* – so your aquarium should either contain fish or plants. Fake plastic fish are quite useless as wealth energizers.

Wealth Luck

Generally there is good fortune for a northwest-facing house all through this year of the water horse. The 8 annual star in the entrance palace brings good news and the luck of the patriarch is consistent through the year. This year luck also favors the matriarch. Women will rise and enjoy significant career successes, especially if they are involved in the communication business. Writers and other creative people will find that their productivity will increase. Recognition brings its own reward.

The most auspicious part of the house is the center, where the 6/8 combination promises wealth luck, as well as harmony in all matters pertaining to relationship luck. This comes from the excellent mountain and water stars. There will be opportunities for making good investments, as well as for getting into upwardly mobile careers.

The east palace has the water star 6, which generally brings good fortune. However, in the east, metal coming into a wood element palace has drawbacks since metal cuts wood.

At the same time, the east plays host this year to the annual 5 star so there could be problems.

Health Luck

We have already seen that the 5 annual star in the east brings afflictions to an otherwise auspicious sector. The 5 attracts severe difficulties to this sector in 2002 and it is a good idea to control it with six-rod windchimes. Another remedy is to place metal coins along the walls of this sector.

The sickness star 2 is in the south. This sector is seriously affected in a negative way by the double 2s here in this south palace. It is a dangerous indication indeed. In the months two and eleven (i.e. March and December) there could be fatal illness as this is when the monthly star 2 flies in. This suggests that the south sector's affliction is serious. I advise that, if this is the natal chart of your house, no one should actually stay in the room that is located in the south. Do take this piece of advice seriously since the potential for contracting a fatal disease – which may have to do with the heart or the kidneys – is very real. Placing an urn of *yin*, or quiet, water in this sector should also disarm the water star 3. Change the water every week so it does not become excessively *yin*.

Relationship Luck

Relationship luck in a northwest 2/3 house is certainly better than that of a northwest 1 house. This is because the mountain star in the entrance palace of northwest is the lucky 7 star. Although the cycle of 7 is now waning as the period comes to a close, nevertheless it means that interpersonal luck for residents with outsiders and business associates in general will be comfortable and cordial.

As for love relationships, the house benefits from the annual 4 flying into the southwest. This is something that benefits everyone, since all houses will likewise enjoy this same phenomenon. In this particular house, however, the southwest does not enjoy good natal chart star numbers. Both the water and mountain stars are not lucky numbers. This means that even if love comes visiting it does not bring happiness.

Love does not have much of a chance, especially if you are living in the southwest sector of the house. Relationships get sabotaged by the conflict of personalities arising from everyday situations.

Prosperous Palaces

The two major sectors of wealth in this house are in the center and the west. These are based on the natal chart numbers. In the center the incidence of the double 7 is most fruitful for the overall luck of the house. In 2002, the northwest sector enjoys the double 8 of the annual star and the *Lo Shu* star. This makes it an auspicious palace.

Generally the wealth luck of the house is not spectacular. However, it should be noted that for 2002 the sector which enjoys the best overall luck – based on an analysis of the annual *Lo Shu* chart – is the northwest. In addition to enjoying the good vibrations of the 8 annual star, this sector is also not afflicted by any bad combinations of stars or other annual afflictions. In view of this it stands to reason that houses that face northwest are most likely to benefit from the good *chi* of that direction.

Dangerous Palaces

All houses are affected by the 5 yellow star, which in 2002 has flown to the east. Unfortunately the east also has the main star 5, and the combination of two 5s can, and usually does, have a deadly effect. This applies to all houses during the year, irrespective of their orientation. In this northwest house, however, the danger from the Five Yellow has been considerably reduced by the presence of the auspicious natal chart numbers. Both mountain and water stars are auspicious in the east. The effect of the Five Yellow is felt most in the months two and eleven (i.e. in March and December), when the monthly 5 also comes visiting the east palace. Anyone with a bedroom located here in the east will surely succumb to illness this year.

The north sector is the area of bad news because the Three Killings resides here this year, as does the annual 3. This is true of all houses so do make certain that you do not undertake renovations in the north. If you must renovate, please choose a good date and make sure you do not begin or end your renovation work in this sector. Renovations undertaken here will be beset by a variety of problems. At the same time, this sector will also cause residents to fall sick or succumb to burglaries and accidents.

The other danger palace is the south, which has the annual 2 star bringing illness. The natal star numbers are also not conducive to having a balanced and harmonious life. Stay wary of the south.

Month-by-Month Analysis

☆ MONTH 1: February 4–March 6

The year starts with the arrival of the fiery monthly 9 star in the northwest. This strengthens the yang/fire nature of the water star in this sector, and combines well with the 8 star – indicating an excellent month for money and business luck. There is growth and abundance for those in business, while career professionals could win a promotion at work. If you reside in this sector of the home you should move forward with courage and determination as luck is on your side. If there are arguments between the older and younger generations of the household, do not let these temporary obstacles slow you down. Move strongly ahead.

The southeast is also good for money luck. Here the combination of 6 with 7 is powerful and excellent for starting a family. This is a good room in which to try for a child this month.

☆ MONTH 2: March 6–April 5

The second month brings stunning good luck to the home, and this will show itself in positive things happening for the patriarch of the household. This happy situation is due to the double 8 star being in the northwest palace. In effect there are altogether three 8 stars here! The other star number, which is the water star of the natal chart, is 9. So the combination is powerful and strong. Wealth luck is present and residents benefit. The only danger is that of excess, since so much good fortune could make one forget that neither good nor bad fortune lasts forever.

The other lucky sector is the center of the house, where the double 7 also brings favorable developments. In the southeast the double 6 exerts its heavenly magic, combining well with the 7 water star. The house is a happy one, as good stars visit the central axis. Note the good numbers in the center line direct beautiful *chi* into the household. Residents should take advantage of this by energizing these central palaces.

☆ MONTH 3: April 5–May 6

This month the monthly 7 star meets the annual 8 star in the northwest, bringing what is known as a "winning hand." The 7/8 combination suggests success in the face of competition. This reading is further strengthened by the presence of the 7 mountain star here. Relationships with outsiders and between family members tend, therefore, to be cordial and warm.

The other palaces of the house are afflicted in some way or other this month. The southeast is visited by the very unlucky 5 and this makes the mountain star 5 in this sector all the more dangerous. Residents living here should hang a six-rod windchime to ensure that misunderstandings do not get out of hand and that illness and accidents do not cause tragedy in the household. The hostile 3 visits the southwest, thereby bringing quarrelsome luck to the women of the family. Note that the natal star numbers here are also inauspicious, so this will be a rather tiresome month – especially for the women of the family. In the north the illness star 2 brings a terrible influence to the annual 3 number here.

☆ MONTH 4: May 6–June 6

Prosperity luck looks up this month. The northwest benefits from the entry of the auspicious monthly 6 star as it combines with the annual 8 to bring good fortune. Luck is excellent and there is good news and good results. This combination of numbers is one of the best. There could be some problems at the office related to annoying politicking by small-minded troublemakers – the Chinese refer to such people as *siew-yan*, meaning "small person." Use a windchime placed strategically at the front of the house to help you dismiss these minor annoyances. The month luck is strong so there is nothing to worry about.

In the southeast the 4 monthly star brings romance luck, which combines brilliantly with the prosperity luck of the annual 6. This is a very promising indication for those who might be contemplating marriage or enlarging the family. Good news comes easily.

☆ MONTH 5: June 6–July 7

A most unpleasant month indeed, made horrible by gossip and bad mouthing. Misunderstandings and quarrels happen on a daily basis caused by the 5 monthly star in the northwest palace and the 3 star in the southeast. This makes the NW/SE axis of the home rather afflicted, as a result of which there is unpleasantness. Residents could also succumb to stomach problems. Expectant mothers should take extra care. Do not move heavy objects and do not sleep in the northwest. This is because the 5 star has flown into the northwest.

Another unlucky palace is the east sector which plays host to the illness star 2. Residents here will fall ill very easily and health is a real problem this month. Those staying here could also be involved in accidents and hurt their heads. Hang plenty of six-rod windchimes here to overcome the afflicted earth energy.

☆ MONTH 6: July 7–August 8

There is favorable news this month, especially for those engaged in the writing and communications professions. Students also enjoy good luck in their studies and exams. The 4 monthly star in the northwest brings that kind of positive energy to the house. At the same time, the 4 star also brings romance and lots of possibilities for happiness. So it is a happy and fulfilling month – just make sure there is no water feature built or placed in the northwest, since this causes romance luck to turn dark and ugly.

Also avoid sleeping in the west palace because the 5 has flown there. The annual 9 star in the west enhances the negative impact of this unfortunate star number.

☆ MONTH 7: August 8–September 8

The number 3 star flies into the northwest this month, bringing with it obstacles caused by difficult people. In feng shui, these troublemakers are known as "devil men" and they make the good energy of the home unpleasant. Progress and success luck comes at the price of betrayal and quarrels. There is gossip and bad tempers all round. Relationships are simply not harmonious because the 3 star afflicts the annual 8 star. If possible, move the children to another room. This is also not a good month to trust anyone.

The lucky sector this month is the southeast. Here the annual 6 star is improved by the entry of the monthly 1 star. This combination brings prosperity and happiness. Note that since the 1 star is of the water element, it is excellent for the southeast sector, which is wood. This suggests that there are opportunities for growth in your business.

In the southwest, money and relationship luck is on a roll as the 8 star enters this palace. Notwithstanding the inauspicious natal stars here, the 8 and 4 is a good combination. The east sector, meanwhile, has become dangerous, so it is a good idea to stay away from this sector. The monthly 9 entering the east palace, where the 5 annual star is located, suggests that the sector has become too inflamed by the fiery 9 star.

☆ MONTH 8: September 8–October 8

In the eighth month the entrance palace – the northwest – is harmed by the illness star 2. Residents will succumb to illness, although there continues to be good money luck. You should hang a six-rod windchime here to control the 2 star number.

The south sector, meanwhile, has the dreaded 2/5 combination of annual and monthly stars, so there is misfortune and extreme bad luck. Illness contracted here this month could be dangerous and may well prove fatal. Move to another room immediately and place metal energy here to keep the bad luck minimal and under control. Note that the inauspicious month and annual stars here overcome the natal stars. This is because we are in the south sector of fire, which feeds the earth. Whenever the 5 and 2 occur together the afflicted earth energy is strengthened, and the best way to exhaust this energy is by using six-rod windchimes.

If you have ever been on the receiving end of a 5 star affliction, you will know how awful it is and how bad the misfortune can be. You will also realize just how effective the six-rod windchime can be in such circumstances.

☆ MONTH 9: October 8–November 7

In the ninth month, the monthly stars of the house have turned friendly. The residents once again experience good fortune as the 1 star flies into the northwest palace and the 8 star flies into the southeast. This means both the front and back of the house benefit from extremely strong energy, and although the center month star 9 is not great, nevertheless, the line stays auspicious because the main star in the center is the number 7.

The sectors to avoid this month are the north and the west. The north is visited by the 5 star, which combines with the hostile 3 and a mountain 2 star. The indications look very negative indeed, so place still water here to contain these bad stars. In the west, the situation is also bad. This is due to the 2 star flying into the sector (note that this 2 is strengthened by the annual 9 star making the west a very negative area indeed). So both sectors bring bad luck to the residents. The indications are that residents simply cannot find success in these two sectors this month. Children will also be negatively affected in these sectors so, if your children are sitting important examinations in this month, move them out of here.

✬ MONTH 10: November 7–December 6

The lucky and unlucky sectors are the same as month one.

✬ MONTH 11: December 7–January 4, 2003

The lucky and unlucky sectors are the same as month two.

✬ MONTH 12: January 5–February 3, 2003

The lucky and unlucky sectors are the same as month three.

How to find your Kua number

Start using this formula by determining your personal auspicious and inauspicious directions. To do this, you will need to work out your personal Kua number. To calculate your Kua number you need your lunar year of birth and your gender. The lunar year of birth is determined by the date of your birth. If you were born between 1 January and 20 February, you need to check the date on which the lunar New Year happened in your year of birth. If you were born before the New Year, subtract one year from your year of birth before calculating your Kua number, so if you were born on 19 January 1966, count your birth year as 1965.

☆ **For men:**

Take your lunar year of birth, add together the last two digits, reduce it to a single number, then subtract this from 10 to get your Kua number.

Example 1: Year of birth 1964 – 6+4=10 and 1+0=1, 10-1= 9.
The Kua number is 9.

Example 2: Year of birth 1984 – 8+4=12 and 1+2=3, 10-3 = 7
so the Kua is 7.

Note: for boys born after 2000, subtract from 9 instead of 10.

☆ **For women:**

Take the lunar year of birth and add together the last two digits, reduce to a single number, and then add 5. If the result is more than 10 reduce to a single digit. The result is your Kua number.

Example 1: Year of birth 1945 – 4+5=9 then 9+5=14, 1+4=5
so the Kua is 5.

Example 2: Year of birth 1982 – 8+2=10 and 1+0=1, 1+5=6
so the Kua is 6.

Are you an East or West group person?

Eight Mansions feng shui explains that everyone is either an East- or a West-group person. Generally, people of the same group tend to be more compatible.

East-group people get along better with other East-group people and the same is true of West-group people. Whether you are an East-group or West-group person depends on your Kua number.

East-group people have the Kua numbers 1, 3, 4, and 9 and their four auspicious directions are north, south, southeast, and east. These are the east group directions and any one of these directions will bring good luck to people in this group.

The good and bad directions

West-group people have the Kua numbers 5, 2, 6, 7, and 8 and for this group the four auspicious directions are west, southwest, northwest, and northeast. If you are a west-group person, any one of these directions will bring you good fortune and good luck.

Now please also take note that East-group directions are inauspicious for West-group people and vice versa. You should commit your Kua number and your auspicious directions to memory so that you will always know your lucky and unlucky directions in any situation. Carry a compass with you always and you can practice this simple feng shui technique wherever you are.

Just knowing if you are East- or West-group allows you to ensure you never face or sleep with your head pointed to an unlucky direction ever again in your life. And as long as you live in a state of awareness of the energy flow in the environment, your chi will always blend harmoniously with that of your space. This implies that you will always make the effort to orientate your sitting and sleeping direction in accordance with your group of lucky directions. Moreover, when you have grown familiar with your directions and have made this awareness a part of your daily habits, you will continually discover fresh uses for the formula. For instance, I always make sure I face my success direction when I am negotiating an important contract, when I am making an important phone call, or when I am giving a lecture or a presentation. Over the years, I like to think of this state of awareness of my living space as one of my success habits. You can do the same. Just remember not to let ease of practice fool you into thinking any less of the formula.